BUSINESS COMMUNICATION

TEN
STEPS
TO
SUCCESS

Lin Lougheed

D1411022

Addison-Wesley Publishing Company, Inc.

Reading, Massachusetts ■ Menlo Park, California ■ New York
Don Mills, Ontario ■ Wokingham, England ■ Amsterdam
Bonn ■ Sydney ■ Singapore ■ Tokyo ■ Madrid ■ San Juan
Paris ■ Seoul ■ Milan ■ Mexico City ■ Taipei

Product Development Director: Judith Bittinger

Executive Editor: Elinor Chamas

Production/Manufacturing: James W. Gibbons

Text Design: Joe di Chiarro

Technical Art: Susan Cronin-Paris

Illustrations: Will Winslow

Cover Design: Will Winslow

The author would like to acknowledge and thank the teachers
and students whose comments and advice refined the text.
The author is especially appreciative of the insightful
suggestions of Bonita Vander, Vice President, Education,
SCS Business and Technical Institute.

**SCS Business and Technical Institutes, New York and
Philadelphia**
Geraldine Jacob, Y. Kokosinski, Robert Nester, Jeanne J.
Newman, Edward Pack, Giovanna Rick, John Sitter

Wilson Adult School, Arlington, VA
Suzanne Grant, Susan Huss, Betty Lynch, Inaam Mansoor,
Sharon McKay, Donna Moss, Kenwyn Schaffner

IDI Editorial Staff and Production Assistants
Anne Kennedy, Gina Richardson, Charles Buck

ISBN: 0-201-51676-4
  3 4 5 6 7 8 9 10 - KE - 97 96 95 94

CONTENTS

To the Student

What is necessary to be a successful business person?

It takes more than learning English words and grammar. You need to know how to use these words. To be successful, you need to know how successful people use these words.

Words express attitudes—attitudes about people, time, office responsibilities, and business relationships. These attitudes differ from culture to culture and from country to country.

Your attitudes influence your actions. By understanding your own attitudes toward business and business relationships, you can better appreciate the attitudes of others. This will help you work more effectively with colleagues from other cultures.

This book will help you:

- organize your time
- read charts and graphs
- write effective letters
- use the telephone effectively
- work as part of a team
- make a good impression
- be a good leader
- expand your vocabulary
- converse more easily

To the Teacher

Business Communication: Ten Steps to Success is written at the intermediate level for students who need English for business purposes. The content of this book is suitable for workplace ESL, adult basic education, or corporate ESL/EFL programs. *Business Communication* presents a carefully structured blend of language skills and the important personal skills required for successful communication in the workplace. Each chapter, or *Step*, contains the following:

A **contents list** that outlines the vocabulary and the functional and language skills that are the focus of the chapter

Two **Case Studies** that let the student analyze and compare two opposing interpersonal styles in a business context

A **How About You** section that lets the student interpret and evaluate his or her own attitudes

Personal Success Skills activities that further develop attitudes and approaches valuable in the business world

Language Skills activities that help the students practice key grammar patterns they will use in actual business situations

Reading and writing exercises that mirror real-life activities, such as scanning the index in a newspaper and writing follow-up letters to customers

Task-based activities, such as **Speak for Yourself** and **Putting It All Together**, that contextualize the language and personal skills of the chapter

Most activities are multipurpose so that students work on content, grammar, basic communication, vocabulary, and critical thinking at the same time. The book is designed to help students learn how words express attitudes that can greatly affect working relationships. As they analyze and develop their own attitudes, they will be moving toward successful business communication.

Be Positive

Case Studies

Making a Bad Impression
Making a Good Impression

Personal Success Skills

Greeting People Positively
Using Positive Body Language
Understanding Cultural Differences

Language Skills

Recognizing Positive and Negative Statements
Interpreting Body Language

Words to Know

appropriate body
  language
(to) make an impression
(to) make eye contact
middle-of-the-road

negative
Personnel Director
positive
response
wrong

Personal Success Hint

Good morning!

Everyone likes a person with a positive attitude. Smile. Look people in the eye. Make a good impression.

Situation: Helen Stewart is a Personnel Director. Tim Carey is looking for a job.

▶ *Circle your answer.*

1. Does Ms. Stewart have a job?	Yes	No	Maybe
2. Does Mr. Carey want a job?	Yes	No	Maybe
3. Will Ms. Stewart give Mr. Carey a job?	Yes	No	Maybe
4. Does Mr. Carey have a positive attitude?	Yes	No	Maybe
5. Does Ms. Stewart have a negative attitude?	Yes	No	Maybe
6. Does Mr. Carey make eye contact with Ms. Stewart?	Yes	No	Maybe
7. Does Ms. Stewart greet Mr. Carey positively?	Yes	No	Maybe
8. Does Mr. Carey respond negatively?	Yes	No	Maybe

How About You?

▶ *Read each sentence and circle your answer.*

1. I say "Good morning" to everyone.	Never	Sometimes	Always
2. I give positive responses to "How are you?"	Never	Sometimes	Always
3. I like my job.	Never	Sometimes	Always
4. I make eye contact.	Never	Sometimes	Always
5. I ask people, "How are you?"	Never	Sometimes	Always
6. I make a good first impression.	Never	Sometimes	Always
7. I remember people's names.	Never	Sometimes	Always
8. I smile.	Never	Sometimes	Always

Situation: Richard Ginns is a Personnel Director. Jane Chapman is looking for a job.

▶ *Circle your answer.*

1. Does Mr. Ginns have a job?　　　　　　　　　　　　　Yes　No　Maybe
2. Does Ms. Chapman want a job?　　　　　　　　　　　Yes　No　Maybe
3. Will Mr. Ginns give Ms. Chapman a job?　　　　　　Yes　No　Maybe
4. Does Ms. Chapman have a positive attitude?　　　　Yes　No　Maybe
5. Does Ms. Chapman make a good first impression?　Yes　No　Maybe
6. Does Ms. Chapman make eye contact with Mr. Ginns?　Yes　No　Maybe

Compare and Discuss

▶ *Compare the case studies.*

1. Who is more positive—Mr. Carey or Ms. Chapman?
2. Who do you want to work with—Mr. Carey or Ms. Chapman?
3. Who do you want to work for—Ms. Stewart or Mr. Ginns?
4. Who has a negative attitude—
   Mr. Carey or Ms. Chapman?
5. Do you ever have little problems? Do you talk
   about them? With whom? When?
6. Rewrite Case Study 1 so that Mr. Carey
   makes a good impression.

Business Hint

You have only ONE chance to make a FIRST impression.

▶ *Look at the different responses:*

Positive Responses	Middle-of-the-Road Responses	Negative Responses
Fine.	Not so bad.	Awful.
Really fine.	So-so.	Terrible.
Never been better.	OK.	Don't ask.
Great.		Horrible.
Terrific.		Not so good.
Very well.		Not so great.
Super.		

▶ *Write if the response is positive, negative, or middle-of-the-road.*

1. Question: How are you?
   Response: Don't ask.   _____

2. Question: How are you?
   Response: Not so good.   _____

3. Question: How are you?
   Response: Terrific.   _____

4. Question: How are you?
   Response: Great.   _____

5. Question: How are you?
   Response: OK.   _____

6. Question: How are you?
   Response: Not too bad.   _____

7. Question: How are you?
   Response: Never been better.   _____

8. Question: How are you?
   Response: Horrible.   _____

Body language is as important as words. Your body can say a lot without words. A smile is positive. A frown is negative.

If you look people in the eye, it is polite.   If you look somewhere else, it is rude.

▶*Answer the question, "How are you?" in different ways.*

Business Hint

In the United States, making eye contact is a sign of honesty.

1. Give a negative response.

   Classmate: How are you today?
   You: **Terrible.** How are you?

2. Give a positive response, but don't look at the person.

   Classmate: How are you today?
   You: **Fine.** How are you?

3. Give a positive response, but don't smile.

   Classmate: How are you today?
   You: **Great.** How are you?

4. Give a positive response, make eye contact, and smile.

   Classmate: How are you today?
   You: **Super, thanks.** How are you?

5. Give a positive response, make eye contact, smile, and offer your hand.

   Classmate: How are you today?
   You: **Really great, thanks.** How are you?

6. Which of the responses above are best for the office? Why? What makes a response positive?

Polite, positive people make a good impression. But every country has a different idea of what is polite.

- In Turkey, your coat should be buttoned when you are with superiors.
- In the Navaho culture, children never make eye contact with their teachers.
- In Mongolia, you shouldn't show someone the bottom of your feet.
- In the United States, it is polite to look people in the eye, to offer your hand, and to smile.

What type of body language is polite in your country?

▶ *Circle your answer. Discuss the results with your classmates.*

	Polite in your country?		**Polite in the U.S.?**	
1. Negative response	Yes	No	Yes	No
2. A smile	Yes	No	Yes	No
3. Eye contact	Yes	No	Yes	No
4. Positive response	Yes	No	Yes	No
5. No eye contact	Yes	No	Yes	No
6. No smile	Yes	No	Yes	No
7. Offering a hand	Yes	No	Yes	No

▶ *Complete these statements about the U.S.*

1. When I give a negative response, I make a _____ impression.
   good/bad

2. When I don't make eye contact, I am _____ in the other person.
   interested/not interested

3. When I don't smile, I make a _____ impression.
   good/bad

4. When I smile, make eye contact, and offer my hand, the other person is

   _____ in me.
   interested/not interested

Speak for Yourself

▶ *Work with a classmate. One of you is Speaker A; the other is Speaker B.*

Speaker A

▶ *Choose a time of day and a positive response. Do the dialogue below.*

Time of Day

morning
afternoon
evening

Positive Response

Fine.
Really fine.
Never been better.
Great.
Terrific.
Very well.
Super.

Speaker A: Good _____. How are
you today?

Speaker B:

Speaker A: I'm just _____, thank
you.

Speaker B

▶ *Choose a positive response and time of day. Do the dialogue below.*

Positive Response

Fine.
Really fine.
Never been better.
Great.
Terrific.
Very well.
Super.

Time of Day

morning
afternoon
evening

Speaker A:

Speaker B: _____ thank you. How
are you this _____?

Speaker A:

▶ *Continue with the other options and practice with your classmate. Switch the roles of Speaker A and Speaker B.*

Positive (+)

I like my job.
I feel fine.
I have a question.

Negative (−)

I **do not** like my job. = I **don't** like my job.
I **do not** feel fine. = I **don't** feel fine.
I **do not** have a question. = I **don't** have a question.

▶*Change the sentences from negative to positive.*

1. I do not want a job. _____

2. I do not understand. _____

3. I do not work hard. _____

4. I don't know your name. _____

5. I don't make eye contact. _____

6. I don't sleep well at night. _____

7. I don't smile. _____

▶*Change the sentences from negative to positive. Change each underlined word to a positive word.*

1. My job is so-so. _____

2. This office is OK. _____

3. I make a bad impression. _____

4. My co-workers are not so bad. _____

5. The Personnel Director is terrible. _____

6. My health is not so good. _____

7. My attitude is awful. _____

▶ *Are these examples of body language positive or negative?*
Circle + or -.

Making eye contact
+ -

Tired
+ -

Smiling
+ -

Frowning
+ -

Energetic
+ -

Inattentive
+ -

Inappropriately
dressed
+ -

Appropriately
dressed
+ -

Avoiding eye contact
+ -

Attentive
+ -

Putting It All Together

Being Positive

1. Write down the name of a friend (or your city or your country). How many positive things can you write about your friend?

2. Write your name on a piece of paper (or write the name of your school, the town you live in, the street you shop on, etc.). Pass the paper around the room. Everyone must write one positive comment about you (or your school, your town, a street, etc.).

3. Outside of class, ask five people, "How are you today?" Write their responses. Are their responses positive or negative?

You:	How are you today?		
Person 1:	_____	Positive	Negative

You:	How are you today?		
Person 2:	_____	Positive	Negative

You:	How are you today?		
Person 3:	_____	Positive	Negative

You:	How are you today?		
Person 4:	_____	Positive	Negative

You:	How are you today?		
Person 5:	_____	Positive	Negative

4. Which person(s) used positive body language? _____

5. Which person(s) made eye contact? _____

6. Which person(s) showed they were interested in you? _____

Step 1 Summary

- Smile.
- Make eye contact.
- Be attentive.
- Be positive.

Be Thoughtful

Case Studies

Losing a Potential Customer
Impressing a Potential Customer

Personal Success Skills

Introducing Yourself
Remembering Names

Language Skills

Recognizing Question Types
Reading Follow-up Letters
Writing Follow-up Letters

Personal Success Hint

Hello, Claire. How are you today?

When you say a person's name, you tell the person: "YOU ARE IMPORTANT!" You are important to me; I remember your name. I am interested in you.

Words to Know

alphabet	logo
business card	potential customer
(to) clarify	(to) recognize
flowchart	(to) remember
follow up	salesman

Situation: Bill Smith is a salesperson for ABC Motors. Mary Kent is a potential customer. She wants to buy a new car.

▶*Circle your answer.*

1. What is the salesperson's first name?	Bill	Mary
2. What is the customer's first name?	Bill	Mary
3. What is the salesperson's last name?	Smith	Kent
4. What is the customer's last name?	Smith	Kent
5. Does Mr. Smith remember Ms. Kent's name?	Yes	No
6. Does Ms. Kent remember Mr. Smith's name?	Yes	No
7. Does Mr. Smith recognize Ms. Kent?	Yes	No
8. Does Ms. Kent recognize Mr. Smith?	Yes	No

Business Idioms and Common Expressions

I'm bad with names. = I can't remember names.
I'm good with faces. = I always remember a face.

How About You?

▶*Circle your answer. Explain your answer.*

1. Are you good with names?	Yes	No	Sometimes
2. Are you good with faces?	Yes	No	Sometimes
3. Is it important to remember names?	Yes	No	Sometimes
4. Is it important to remember faces?	Yes	No	Sometimes

Situation: Jack Barnes sells computers. Bob Wright needs a new computer. He was in Mr. Barnes' store last week. Mr. Barnes sees Mr. Wright on the street.

▶*Circle your answer.*

1. What is the salesperson's first name?	Bob	Jack
2. What is the customer's last name?	Barnes	Wright
3. Does Mr. Barnes remember Mr. Wright's name?	Yes	No
4. Does Mr. Wright remember Mr. Barnes' name?	Yes	No
5. Is Mr. Barnes a positive person?	Yes	No
6. Does Mr. Barnes use Mr. Wright's name often?	Yes	No

Compare and Discuss

▶*Compare the case studies.*

1. Who is a better salesman? Jack Barnes or Bill Smith? Why?
2. Which customer is more pleased? Mary Kent or Bob Wright? Why?
3. Who would you buy something from? Mr. Smith or Mr. Barnes? Why?
4. Do you ever forget a name? If yes, how does it make you feel? Embarrassed? Apologetic? Unconcerned?
5. Has anyone forgotten your name? How did you feel? Embarrassed? Angry? Unconcerned?

Don't be shy. Let people know who you are. Introduce yourself to strangers.

Mark Grant: Hello. My name is Mark Grant.

Bob Grodosky: Nice to meet you, Mr. Grant. My name is Bob Grodosky.

Mark Grant: It's a pleasure, Mr. Grodosky.

▶ *Introduce yourself to the people around you in the classroom. Don't forget to look them in the eye and smile.*

Speaker A: Hello. My name is _____.
                                A's Name

Speaker B: Hi. _____.
                  Mr./Mrs./Ms. A's Name

             I'm _____.
                  B's Name

Speaker A: I'm pleased to meet you,
             _____.
              Mr./Mrs./Ms. B's Name

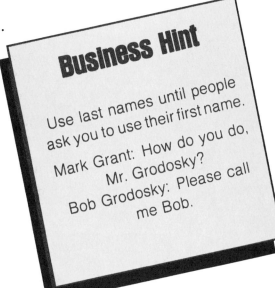

Business Hint

Use last names until people ask you to use their first name.

Mark Grant: How do you do, Mr. Grodosky?

Bob Grodosky: Please call me Bob.

Use a person's name right away. When you say a name often, you will remember it.

▶ *Complete the conversations.*

1. Jane Quinn: Good evening. My name is Quinn, Jane Quinn.
   Rob Jennings: Hello, Ms. _____. I'm Rob Jennings.
   Jane Quinn: Nice to meet you, Mr. _____.

2. Mark Hopkins: Let me introduce myself. Mark Hopkins.
   Karen White: Good evening, _____. I'm pleased to meet you. My name is Karen White.
   Mark Hopkins: I'm pleased to meet you, _____.

Ask for clarification. If you don't understand a name, ask the person to repeat it or spell it out loud.

▶ *Complete the conversation.*

Martha Kent:	My name is Kent. Martha Kent.
Ron Goodman:	I'm sorry. What is your last name?
Martha Kent:	_____.
Ron Goodman:	Kent. How do you spell Kent?
Martha Kent:	_____.

▶ *Practice with a classmate.*

Speaker A: My name is _____.

Speaker B: I'm sorry. What is your | last name?
| first name?

Speaker A: | (Last name).
| (First name).

Speaker B: How do you spell your | last name?
| first name?
| that name?

Speaker A: _____.

Spelling for Clarification

Some letters sound alike when we spell. For example, *B* sounds like *D*.

Bob Bolt: My last name is Bolt.

Julie Robins: Pleased to meet you, Mr. Dolt.

Bob Bolt: That's Bolt with a B as in "boy."

Julie Robins: Oh, I'm sorry, Mr. Bolt.

To clarify, it's a good idea to ask:

"B as in boy, or D as in dog?"

Do people sometimes confuse letters in your name when they spell it? You may need to give examples.

▶ *Look at the following examples of spelling clarification. Add more examples.*

A as in Alpha, _____ , _____ N as in November, _____ , _____

B as in Bravo, _____ , _____ O as in Oscar, _____ , _____

C as in Charlie, _____ , _____ P as in Paper, _____ , _____

D as in Delta, _____ , _____ Q as in Quebec, _____ , _____

E as in Echo, _____ , _____ R as in Romeo, _____ , _____

F as in Foxtrot, _____ , _____ S as in Sierra, _____ , _____

G as in Golf, _____ , _____ T as in Tango, _____ , _____

H as in Hotel, _____ , _____ U as in Uniform, _____ , _____

I as in India, _____ , _____ V as in Victor, _____ , _____

J as in Juliette, _____ , _____ W as in Whiskey, _____ , _____

K as in Kilo, _____ , _____ X as in X-ray, _____ , _____

L as in Lima, _____ , _____ Y as in Yankee, _____ , _____

M as in Mike, _____ , _____ Z as in Zulu, _____ , _____

▶Practice with your classmates.

Speaker A: My last name is | Braun.
Tracy.
Como.
Feder.

Speaker B: Pleased to meet you, Mr. | Braum.
Gracy.
Coma.
Beder.

Speaker A: That's | Braun
Tracy | with | an N
a   T | as in | November.
Tango.
Como | an O | Oscar.
Feder | an F | Foxtrot.

Speaker B: Oh, I'm sorry, Mr. | Braun.
Tracy.
Como.
Feder.

See the name written. To remember a name, it helps to see it written. You can ask for a business card, or you can write down the name and phone number.

Bob Wilson: Do you have a card?

Julie Robins: No, I'm sorry. I'm out of cards.

Bob Wilson: Let me write down your name and number.

▶Practice with your classmates.

1. Practice with cards.

   Speaker A: Do you have a card?

   Speaker B: Yes, here you are.

   Speaker A: Thank you. Here's mine.

2. Practice without cards.

   Speaker A: Do you have a card?

   Speaker B: No, I'm sorry. I don't.
   No, I'm sorry. I'm out of cards.

   Speaker A: Let me write down your name and number.

Associate the name with something. To remember a person's name, write something about the person on his or her business card.

▶ *These people gave Bill Smith their cards. Help Bill remember their names.*

| Mark Grant | Jane Quinn | Rob Jennings | Julie Robins | Bob Grodosky |

1. Who has long, black hair? _____

2. Who is wearing a bowtie? _____

3. Who has a beard? _____

4. Who was at the hotel? _____

5. Who has long blond hair? _____

▶ *Write something about the person on his or her business card.*

Mark Grant
Architect
Smith, Jones, and Grant

111 Main Street Suite 2
Anytown, California
555-1234

$ Fast Money, Inc.

512 Big Bucks Drive
Dollarville, Michigan
555-3400

Jane Quinn
Stock Broker

Rob Jennings, Salesperson

Best Products ★

123 Quality Way • Acme, PA
555-9908

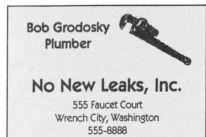

Bob Grodosky
Plumber

No New Leaks, Inc.

555 Faucet Court
Wrench City, Washington
555-8888

Julie Robins, Realtor
House and Home Sales

1212 Condo Circle
Hometown, Iowa
555-6432

Speak for Yourself

Work with a classmate. One of you is Speaker A; the other is Speaker B.

Speaker A

▶ *Choose a name and do the dialogue below.*

First Names		Last Names
Male	**Female**	
Bob	Mary	Smith
Fred	Sue	Brown
Sam	Lynn	Green
Tom	Helen	Wilson
Tim	Pam	Duffy
Bill	Karen	Haley

Speaker A: Hello. My name is

_____

Speaker B:

Speaker A: I'm sorry. What is your last name?

Speaker B:

Speaker A: How do you spell that?

Speaker B:

Speaker A: _____

Speaker B:

Speaker A: No, I'm sorry. I'm out of cards.

Speaker B:

Speaker B

▶ *Choose a name and do the dialogue below.*

First Names		Last Names
Male	**Female**	
Jack	Anne	Madison
John	Kate	Franklin
Dick	Jane	Washington
Mike	Lisa	Harrison
George	Judy	Lincoln

Speaker A:

Speaker B: It's a pleasure to meet you,

_____. I'm

_____

Speaker A:

Speaker B:_____

Speaker A:

Speaker B: _____

How do you spell YOUR last name?

Speaker A:

Speaker B: Do you have a card?

Speaker A:

Speaker B: Let me write down your name and number.

▶ *Use another name and do the dialogue again.*

Yes/No Questions with "be"

▶ *Look at the models:*

Speaker A thinks: *(Is he an accountant?)*

Speaker A asks: **Are you** an accountant?

Speaker B says: Yes, **I am.**

Speaker A thinks: *(Is he from the United States?)*

Speaker A asks: **Are you** from the United States?

Speaker B says: No, **I'm not.**

▶*Write the question you want to ask. Ask your classmate.*

1. You think: *(Is she good with faces?)*

   You ask: _____

2. You think: *(Is he from Egypt?)*

   You ask: _____

3. You think: *(Is she the new secretary?)*

   You ask: _____

4. You think: *(Is he studying English?)*

   You ask: _____

5. You think: *(Is he a salesman?)*

   You ask: _____

Yes/No Questions with "do"

▶ *Look at the models:*

You think: *(Does he remember names well?)*

You ask: **Do you** remember names well?

Speaker B: Yes, **I do.**

You think: *(Does he know how to spell my name?)*

You ask: **Do you** know how to spell my name?

Speaker B: No, **I don't.**

▶ *Write the question you want to ask. Ask your classmate.*

1. You think: *(Does he speak Chinese?)*

   You ask: _____

2. You think: *(Does she study English?)*

   You ask: _____

3. You think: *(Does she have a job?)*

   You ask: _____

4. You think: *(Does he like his work?)*

   You ask: _____

5. You think: *(Does she have a business card?)*

   You ask: _____

"Wh" Questions

▶ *Look at the models:*

You think: *(Where is he from?)*

You ask: **Where are you from?**

Speaker B: **I'm from** Argentina.

You think: *(What does she study?)*

You ask: **What do you study?**

Speaker B: **I study** Management.

▶ *Write the question you want to ask. Ask your classmate.*

1. You think: *(Where does he work?)*

   You ask: _____

2. You think: *(What does she do?)*

   You ask: _____

3. You think: *(How does she spell her name?)*

   You ask: _____

4. You think: *(When does she work?)*

   You ask: _____

5. You think: *(Where does he study?)*

   You ask: _____

Help people remember your name. After you meet someone,
write to him or her. This letter is called a follow-up letter.

Situation: Ken Woods sells photocopiers. Charles Watts is a potential customer. Ken writes Charles Watts a follow-up letter.

Central Photocopiers
345 West Broadway
New York, NY 10007
212-553-4545

January 18, 1993

Mr. Charles Watts
Acme Machine Works
1230 Central Street
Newstown, Connecticut 20007

Dear Mr. Watts:

Thank you for coming to our store yesterday and looking
at our new photocopiers. If you have any questions,
please call me.

Sincerely yours,

Ken Woods

▶ *Circle your answer to each question.*

1. Who wrote the letter?	Ken Woods	Charles Watts
2. Who was the letter written to?	Ken Woods	Charles Watts
3. Who is looking for a photocopier?	Ken Woods	Charles Watts
4. Who is a potential customer?	Ken Woods	Charles Watts
5. Who is a salesperson?	Ken Woods	Charles Watts

Follow-up Letter 1

Situation: Claudia Jackson sells computer printers. Christine Norton is a potential customer. Claudia writes Christine a letter.

▶ *Complete the follow-up letter using these words:*

looking   printers   questions   you   store

Power **P**rinters
4070 Silicon Avenue
Sunnyvale, CA 987544

February 21, 1994

Ms. Christine Norton
5151 Short Lane
Santa Clara, CA 97777

Dear Ms. Norton:

Thank_____ for coming to our _____ yesterday and

_____ at our new _____. If you have any

_____, please call me.

Sincerely yours,

Claudia Jackson

Follow-up Letter 2

Situation: Bob Wright sells computers. Jack Barnes is a potential customer. Bob writes Jack Barnes a letter.

▶ *Complete the follow-up letter using these words:*

Barnes	coming	have	our	you
call	computers	looking	questions	yours

Energo Computers
442 Walton Drive
Reading, Massachusetts 01845

February 21, 1994

Mr. Jack _____
18 South Street
Reading, Massachusetts 01845

Dear Mr. Barnes:

Thank _____ for _____ to our store yesterday and

_____ at _____ new _____. If you

_____ any _____ , please _____.

Sincerely _____ ,

Bob Wright

Follow-up Letter 3

Situation: You sell fax machines. Your classmate called you about your fax machines.

▶ *Write him or her a letter. Use your own paper.*

Putting It All Together

Remembering Names

1. Write the personal success skill that matches the conversation for Tony Conroy.

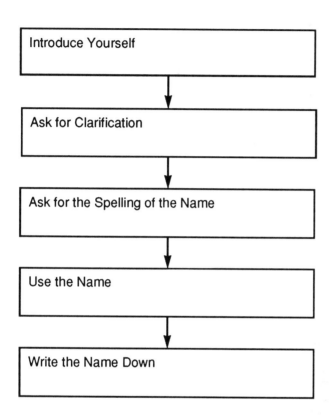

Introduce Yourself

Ask for Clarification

Ask for the Spelling of the Name

Use the Name

Write the Name Down

Tony Conroy:	Hi. I'm Tony Conroy. _____
Bill Madsen:	Hello. My name is Bill Madsen.
Tony Conroy:	I'm sorry. What is your last name? _____
Bill Madsen:	Madsen.
Tony Conroy:	Madsen. How do you spell that? _____
Bill Madsen:	M-A-D-S-E-N.
Tony Conroy:	Do you have a card, Mr. Madsen? _____
Bill Madsen:	No, I'm sorry, I don't.
Tony Conroy:	Let me write down your name and number. _____

2. Introduce yourself to a classmate. Follow the flowchart on page 25. If you don't have business cards, make some. Cut a sheet of paper into 15 rectangles and write your name and address on each rectangle. Design a logo, too!

3. Exchange cards with your classmates. Write something about them on the front or back of the cards.

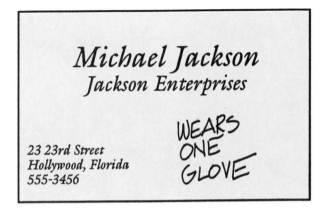

4. You are a salesperson. Your classmate comes in to buy something. Introduce yourself. Follow up with a letter.

Step 2 Summary

- Remember names and faces.
- Don't be shy.
- Ask for clarification.
- Ask for business cards.
- Write follow-up letters.

Be a Team Player

Case Studies

Making New Colleagues Feel Uneasy
Making New Colleagues Feel Welcome

Personal Success Skills

Being Aware of the Corporate Structure
Learning What Your Colleagues Do

Language Skills

Using Articles *a* and *the* Correctly
Recognizing Prepositions
Reading a Company Directory
Writing Thank-you Notes

Personal Success Hint

Thanks for your report, Jim. We make a good team!

To be a success, you must know your business well. But you also must learn how you can work as part of the team. Be a good team player.

Words to Know

ambitious	jealous
(to) be in charge	organized
busy	position
colleague	purchasing
directory	successful
employee	supervisor
exchange	
extension	

Situation: David Hunter has worked for Holiday Travel for 15 years. He is a Purchasing Clerk. He wants to be the Director of Purchasing someday. George Monroe is a new employee. He's a Purchasing Clerk, too. It's his first day on the job.

▶ *Circle your answer.*

1. Mr. Monroe is a new employee.	Yes	No	Maybe
2. Mr. Hunter is Mr. Monroe's supervisor.	Yes	No	Maybe
3. Mr. Hunter wants to be the Purchasing Director.	Yes	No	Maybe
4. Mr. Hunter is a positive person.	Yes	No	Maybe
5. Mr. Hunter is a friendly person.	Yes	No	Maybe
6. Mr. Hunter is well-liked.	Yes	No	Maybe
7. Mr. Hunter doesn't want Mr. Monroe to be successful.	Yes	No	Maybe
8. Mr. Hunter wants to control Mr. Monroe.	Yes	No	Maybe
9. Mr. Hunter is a team player.	Yes	No	Maybe
10. Mr. Hunter is successful.	Yes	No	Maybe

How About You?

▶ *Circle your answer. Explain your answer.*

Which of these adjectives describe you?

1. Friendly	Yes	No	Sometimes
2. Rude	Yes	No	Sometimes
3. Well-liked	Yes	No	Sometimes
4. Lonely	Yes	No	Sometimes
5. Ambitious	Yes	No	Sometimes
6. Cooperative	Yes	No	Sometimes
7. Jealous	Yes	No	Sometimes
8. Busy	Yes	No	Sometimes
9. Successful	Yes	No	Sometimes
10. A team player	Yes	No	Sometimes

Situation: Ron Howard has worked for the East West Trade Company for 10 years. He is the Assistant Manager for Pacific Sales. He wants to be Vice-President of International Sales. Mark Curtis is a new employee. He will work with Mr. Howard. It's his first day on the job.

▶*Circle your answer.*

1. Mr. Curtis is a new employee.	Yes	No	Maybe
2. Mr. Curtis is Mr. Howard's boss.	Yes	No	Maybe
3. Mr. Howard's position is higher than Mr. Curtis' position.	Yes	No	Maybe
4. Mr. Howard is a positive person.	Yes	No	Maybe
5. Mr. Howard is a friendly person.	Yes	No	Maybe
6. Mr. Howard is successful.	Yes	No	Maybe
7. Mr. Howard doesn't want Mr. Curtis to be successful.	Yes	No	Maybe

Compare and Discuss

▶*Compare the case studies.*

1. Who is a friendlier colleague—David Hunter or Ron Howard? Why?
2. Who feels more comfortable—George Monroe or Mark Curtis? Why?
3. Why doesn't Mr. Hunter want Mr. Monroe to talk to the other workers?
4. Who would you like to work with—Mr. Hunter or Mr. Howard?
5. Why is it important to be a good team player?

An organizational chart shows the different positions in
a company. The organizational chart shows:

    1) who supervises and
    2) who reports to a supervisor.

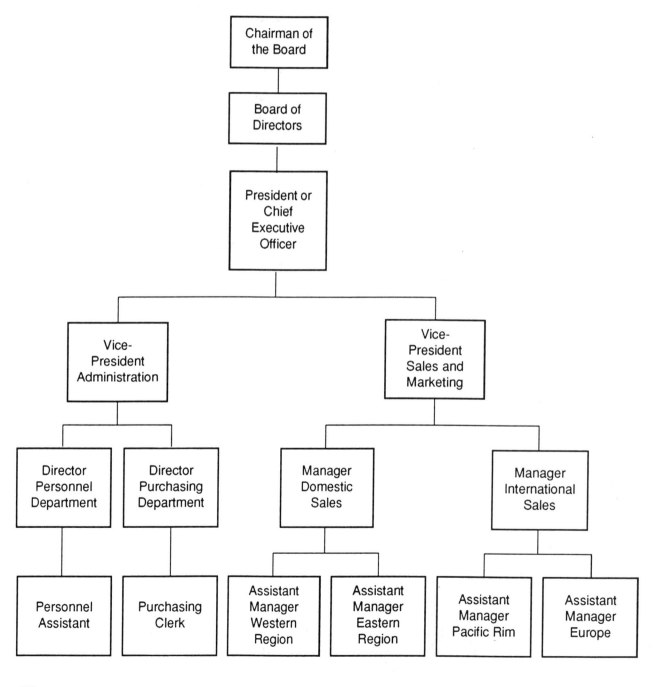

▶ *Circle the answer. Use the organizational chart on page 30.*

1. Who reports to the Director of the Personnel Department?

   a. Purchasing Clerk   b. Personnel Assistant

2. Who reports to the Vice President of Sales and Marketing?

   a. Personnel Assistant   b. Manager, Domestic Sales

3. Who reports to the Director of the Purchasing Department?

   a. Vice-President, Sales and Marketing   b. Purchasing Clerk

4. Who supervises the Assistant Sales Manager in charge of Europe?

   a. Manager, International Sales   b. Manager, Domestic Sales

5. Who supervises the Purchasing Clerk?

   a. Director, Personnel   b. Director, Purchasing

▶ *Work with a classmate. Look at the organizational chart on page 30. Write the name of the position in the blank.*

1. I am in charge of the company. Everyone reports to me. I make all the final decisions. I'm the _____.

2. All of the sales personnel in Europe report to me. The Manager of International Sales supervises me. I'm the _____.

3. My supervisor is responsible for all purchases made by the company. I complete the forms for him to sign. I'm the _____.

4. I help all new employees with their forms for health insurance, pay checks, and other employment benefits. I'm the _____.

5. The Directors of Personnel and Purchasing report to me, and I report to the Chief Executive Officer. I make sure the company runs efficiently. I'm the

   _____.

There are several ways to ask a person's profession:

What do you do? = What is your position? = What is your job?

Where do you work? = What company do you work for? = Which department do you work in?

▶ *Look at this model:*

Julie Chang: Where do you work?

Bob Wilson: I work for **Preston Supplies Company.**

▶ *Practice with your classmates.*

Person A: Where do you work?

Person B: I work for
Deluxe Car Rental.
Capitol Limousine Service.
Empire Glass Company.
JK Business Systems.
Euro-American Shipping Company.
Executive Office Group.

▶ *Look at this model:*

Julie Chang: What do you do?

Bob Wilson: I'm the **Personnel Director.**

▶ *Practice with your classmates.*

Person A: What do you do?

Person B: I'm the
Personnel Director.
Sales Manager.
President.
Assistant Manager.
Administrative Assistant.
Chairman of the Board.
Chief Executive Officer.

Business Hint

In some companies the Personnel Director is called the Human Resources Director.

Use the article *a* when there are many examples of something.

Speaker A:　What does he do?

Speaker B:　He's **a** typist.

Use the article *the* when there is only one example of something.

Speaker A:　What does she do?

Speaker B:　She's **the** Marketing Director.

▶ *Write* a *or* the *to complete the sentences.*

1. What does she do?

   She's ＿＿＿＿＿＿ purchasing clerk. (There are many purchasing clerks.)

2. What is your position?

   I'm ＿＿＿＿＿＿ Personnel Director. (There is only one personnel director.)

3. What is his job?

   He's ＿＿＿＿＿＿ Chief Executive Officer (There is only one chief executive officer.)

4. What do you do?

   I'm ＿＿＿＿＿＿ vice-president. (There are many vice-presidents.)

5. What is her position?

   She's ＿＿＿＿＿＿ sales manager. (There are many sales managers.)

▶ *Write* a *or* the *to complete the sentences. Use the Organizational Chart on page 30 to answer these questions.*

1. What do you do?

   I'm ＿＿＿＿＿＿ Chairman of the Board.

2. What do you do?

   I'm ＿＿＿＿＿＿ Director of Personnel.

3. What do you do?

   I'm ＿＿＿＿＿＿ manager.

4. What do you do?

   I'm ＿＿＿＿＿＿ Purchasing Clerk.

Business Idioms and Common Expressions

Where does he work? = What company does he work for?
                    = Which department does he work in?

Use *for* or *at* to describe a company.

Speaker A: Where does she work?

Speaker B: She works **for** United Travel Company.

             She works **at** United Travel Company.

Use *in* to describe a department.

Speaker A: Where does he work?

Speaker B: He works **in** the International Sales Department.

▶ *Write* for, at, *or* in *to complete the sentences.*

1. Where do you work?

   I work _____ the Purchasing Department.

2. Where does she work?

   She works _____ World Computers, Inc.

3. Which department do you work in?

   I work _____ the Administration Department.

4. Where does he work?

   He works _____ the Sales Department.

5. What company do you work for?

   I work _____ Universal Foods.

6. Where do they work?

   They work _____ ABC Machine Company.

Speak for Yourself

▶ *Work with a classmate. One of you is Speaker A; the other is Speaker B.*

Speaker A	**Speaker B**
▶ *Choose a company and position. Then do the dialogue below.*	▶ *Choose a company and position. Then do the dialogue below.*

Speaker A

Companies:
Harmony Music Company
Tasty Vegetables
Education Systems
First Rate Copiers

Positions:
Manager of Sales
Personnel Director
President
Assistant Manager
Administrative Assistant

Speaker B

Companies:
Regina Carpets
Carter's Tools
Northwood Department Store
Pools Unlimited

Positions:
Assistant Manager
Director of Sales
Vice-President
Secretary
Director of Research
Chairman of the Board
Chief Executive Officer

Speaker A.   My name is _____.
                                                 name

Speaker B:

Speaker A: I'm sorry. What do you do?

Speaker B:

Speaker A: I'm _____.
                               position + company

Speaker A:

Speaker B: Hello, _____. My
                                       name
name is _____.
                         name
I'm _____.
            position

Speaker A:

Speaker B: I'm _____. Where do
                           position
you work?

Speaker A:

▶ *Continue with the other options and practice with your classmate. Switch the roles of Speaker A and Speaker B.*

Kral Computers Directory

Name	Position	Phone No.	Name	Position	Phone No.
Rosie Grady	Secretary, Personnel	998-3208	Anne-Marie Tiburon	Salesperson, Europe	998-3452
Mark Hamson	Director, Personnel Dept.	998-3203	Wilson Vaughn	Assistant Director, Administration	998-3340
Grace Keeler	Purchasing Clerk	998-3554	James Wilson	Manager, Domestic Sales	998-3450
Julie Kent	Assistant Manager, Marketing	998-3462	Ken Wrightsman	Assistant Manager, Sales	998-3456
Macey Price	Secretary, Sales	998-3478	Mel Zelner	Secretary, Administration	998-3349
Carl Stone	Personnel Clerk	998-3209			

Business Idioms and Common Expressions

In a telephone number, the first three digits are the exchange.
The last four digits are the extension.

998-3208

exchange extension

▶ *Circle the letter of the correct answer.*

1. A computer paper salesperson wants to make a contact. Who does he or she contact?
   a. The Purchasing Department   b. The Sales Department

   What extension should the sales person call?
   a. 3554   b. 3208

2. A secretary wants a job. Who does he or she contact?
   a. The Purchasing Department   b. The Personnel Department

   What extension should the secretary call?
   a. 3209   b. 3450

3. James Wilson is out of town. Who does he call for his messages?
   a. The secretary in Sales   b. The Manager of Sales

   What extension should Mr. Wilson call?
   a. 3478   b. 3462

4. The air conditioning does not work in the building. Who should you call?
   a. The Administration Department   b. The Purchasing Department

   What extension should you call?
   a. 3349   b. 3209

5. The telephone exchange for Kral Computers is
   a. 998   b. 3450

6. The extensions for the Sales Department begin with
   a. 34   b. 33

7. The extensions for the Personnel Department begin with
   a. 32   b. 33

8. The extensions for the Purchasing Department begin with
   a. 35   b. 32

Language Skill — Writing Thank-you Notes

You should follow up a special event with a thank-you note within 24 hours.

Thank-you Note 1

Situation: Mr. Smith invited Mrs. Pomeroy to a reception at the company's new offices.

Mable Pomeroy

29 Bucks Lane
Deer Glade, North Carolina 30303

September 16, 1994

Mr. Frank C. Smith
Smith Services, Inc.
Tricity Industrial Park
Durham, NC 30303-4444

Dear Mr. Smith:

It was very nice of you to invite me to your reception last night. I enjoyed the chance to see your beautiful new offices and to talk with you again.

Thank you for your kind invitation. Best wishes for the future.

Sincerely yours,

Mable Pomeroy

Thank-you Note 2

Situation: Mr. White introduced Mr. James Malone to a potential customer.

▶ *Complete the note with these words.*

    Best   introduce   order   you   yours

 Better Widget Company
2020 North First Street ◆ Birmingham, Alabama 40405

October 12, 1994

Mr. Cleveland L. White
White Supplies, Inc.
1456 Main Street
Selma, AL 41567

Dear Mr. White:

It was very nice of you to _____ me to Helen Jones.

She is interested in seeing our new product and may

_____ 1,000 units.

Thank _____ for your sales lead. _____wishes

for the future.

                  Sincerely _____ ,

                  James Malone

Thank-you Note 3

Situation: Mrs. Gringold invited a client, Mrs. Rosalind Prince, to a seminar
on improving your telephone skills.

▶ *Complete the note with these words.*

Dear	invitation	nice	Thank	chance
future	last	Sincerely	the	

Rosalind Prince
49 Luck Lane • Norman, OK 87450

September 16, 1995

Hermoine Gringold
Gringold Consulting Company
9 Franklin Place, Suite 4
Norman, OK 87450

_____ Mrs. Gringold:

It was very _____ of you to invite me to

_____ seminar _____ night. I enjoyed the chance

to learn about telephone skills and the _____ to

talk with you again.

_____ you for your kind _____ and best wishes for

the _____ .

_____ yours,

Rosalind Prince

Thank-you Note 4

Situation: Mr. Easton invited you to a workshop on remembering names.

▶ *Write a thank-you note to Mr. Easton. Use your own paper.*

Putting It All Together

Getting Organized

1. Make an organizational chart for your school, for your own company, or for a company you know about. Present the chart to the class and tell what each person on your chart does.

2. Ask all of your classmates to spell their names and give their phone numbers. Make a telephone directory for your class. Put the names in alphabetical order. Be sure you spell the names correctly.

3. Do your classmates have job titles? Add the job titles and their company names to your directory. Organize this directory by job titles, not by names.

Step 3 Summary

- Make new colleagues feel welcome.
- Learn about your colleagues.
- Know people's titles.
- Write thank-you notes.

Be Interested

Case Studies

Having an Unsuccessful Conversation
Having a Successful Conversation

Personal Success Skills

Making Introductions
Offering Personal Information
Finding Something in Common

Language Skills

Recognizing Question Types
Combining Sentences
Reading a Newspaper Index
Writing Follow-up Notes

Personal Success Hint

How was your weekend, Jane?

People like it when you use their name. They also like you to be interested in them as a person—not just as a "company employee."

Words to Know

announcement
assistant
brochure
get acquainted
have something
  in common
invite
join (someone)
shy
vacation

Situation: Mark Winston wants Sam Tenly to meet Mary Chapin. Mr. Tenly is the Vice-President of European Sales. Ms. Chapin just returned from a three-week visit to the European offices.

▶ *Circle your answer.*

1. Mr. Winston introduced Mr. Tenly to Ms. Chapin.	Yes	No	Maybe
2. Mr. Tenly is shy.	Yes	No	Maybe
3. Ms. Chapin is shy.	Yes	No	Maybe
4. Mr. Winston wants them to talk about sales in Europe.	Yes	No	Maybe
5. Mr. Tenly and Ms. Chapin talk about sales in Europe.	Yes	No	Maybe
6. Mr. Winston is polite.	Yes	No	Maybe
7. Ms. Chapin and Mr. Tenly used each other's names.	Yes	No	Maybe
8. Mr. Winston offered personal information.	Yes	No	Maybe
9. Ms. Chapin and Mr. Tenly have something in common.	Yes	No	Maybe

How About You?

▶ *Circle your answer. Explain your answer.*

When you are with strangers, . . .

1. you introduce yourself.	Yes	No	Sometimes
2. you tell something about yourself.	Yes	No	Sometimes
3. you are shy.	Yes	No	Sometimes
4. you tell something about others.	Yes	No	Sometimes
5. you wait to be introduced.	Yes	No	Sometimes
6. you let the other person start a conversation.	Yes	No	Sometimes
7. you look for things in common.	Yes	No	Sometimes

Situation: Bill Revson, a potential client, is visiting from Toronto. Tom Patterson is introducing him to the employees of the company.

▶ *Circle your answer.*

1. Mr. Patterson introduced Mr. Revson to Ms. Steele.	Yes	No	Maybe
2. Mr. Revson is interested.	Yes	No	Maybe
3. Ms. Steele is interested.	Yes	No	Maybe
4. Mr. Patterson wants them to talk about golf.	Yes	No	Maybe
5. Mr. Patterson wants them to talk about Toronto.	Yes	No	Maybe
6. Mr. Patterson is polite.	Yes	No	Maybe
7. Ms. Steele and Mr. Revson used each other's names.	Yes	No	Maybe

Compare and Discuss

▶ *Compare the case studies.*

1. Who makes better introductions—Mr. Winston or Mr. Patterson? Why?
2. Who feels more comfortable—Mr. Revson or Ms. Chapin?
3. Who is more interested—Mr. Tenly or Ms. Steele?
4. What did Mr. Revson and Ms. Steele have in common?
5. What did Mr. Tenly and Ms. Chapin have in common?
6. How could Mr. Winston help Mr. Tenly and Ms. Chapin get acquainted?

Here are two rules for making introductions:

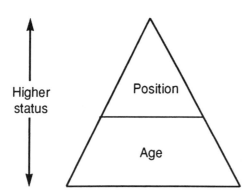

Higher status

A lower ranking employee is introduced to a higher ranking employee.

A younger person is introduced to an older person.

▶ *Look at this model.*

Situation: Mrs. Margaret Perry is the President of Computer, Inc. She is 45 years old. Mr. John Smith is a new salesperson. He is 25 years old.

Ted Conran:	Mrs. Perry, I'd like you to meet Mr. John Smith, a new salesperson with our company. Mr. Smith, this is Mrs. Margaret Perry, the President of our Company.
Margaret Perry:	How do you do, Mr. Smith?
John Smith:	How do you do, Ms. Perry? It's nice to meet you.

▶ *Complete the introduction.*

1. Ms. Jones is a retired accountant. She is 60 years old.
   Mr. Brown is Director of Sales. He is 45 years old.

   _____, I'd like you to meet _____. _____ this is _____.

2. Mr. Smith is Marketing Manager. He is 30 years old.
   Mr. Williams is a major shareholder. He is 80 years old.

   _____, I'd like you to meet _____. _____ this is _____.

3. Ms. Wright is a member of the Board of Directors. She is 30 years old.
   Mr. Reed is Vice-President of International Sales. He is 55 years old.

   _____, I'd like you to meet _____. _____ this is _____.

▶ *Practice with two of your classmates.*

Speaker A: _____, I'd like you to meet _____. _____ this is

   _____.

Speaker B: How do you do, _____?

Speaker C: How do you do, _____? It's nice to meet you.

When you introduce people, provide some personal information. This will start the conversation. You can provide a job title or tell something about personal interests.

▶ *Look at this model.*

Ted Conran: Mrs. Perry is our President. She's a great tennis player.

Margaret Perry: What do you do, Mr. Smith?

John Smith: I'm a sales manager in the Pacific Rim. I like tennis, too!

▶ *Practice with two of your classmates.*

Speaker A: _____ is the Manager of the International Sales Department.
                      student's name
                _____ is interested in _____.
                  He/She

Speaker B: What do you do?

Speaker C: I'm the new | Personnel Director. | I like _____, too!

| |
| Personnel Director. |
| Assistant Manager. |
| Director of Sales. |
| Vice-President. |
| Secretary. |
| Director of Research. |
| Chairman of the Board. |
| Chief Executive Officer. |

When you meet someone, try to find a common interest. Do you both play golf? Do you both have children in school? Do you take the same bus to work? Do you live near each other?

Frank: Where are you going for your vacation?

Jeff: I'm going to London.

Frank: London's a great city. I went last year!

Which sentence shows that the speakers have something in common? What might come next in the conversation?

▶ *Which response shows that the speakers have something in common? Circle your answer.*

1. John: I'm playing golf this weekend.
   Jerry: a. Next weekend let's play at my club.
   b. I'm watching TV.

2. Les: I'm going to an Italian restaurant this evening.
   Fay: a. I love Italian food.
   b. I'm getting sick.

3. Ellen: I went to the University of California at Los Angeles.
   Sue: a. I love skiing.
   b. I used to live in California.

4. George: I play tennis before breakfast.
   Mary: a. I eat a big breakfast.
   b. I prefer to play in the evening.

5. Irene: I hate to fly.
   Grant: a. I never feed birds.
   b. Me, too. I always take the train.

Language Skill — Recognizing Question Types

You ask questions to get information.

Question Form	Begins With	Answered By
yes/no	do, can, could would, should is, are, was, were	yes, no
"wh"	who, what, when where, why, how	specific information

Suppose you ask a yes/no question:

Do you like to play basketball?

The answer may be short:

Yes, I do. or *No, I don't.*

Now suppose you ask a "wh" question:

What sports do you like?

The answer will probably be longer:

I like golf, tennis, and basketball.

▶ *Circle the correct answer.*

1. When did you arrive?
   a. At midnight. b. Yes, last night. c. No, I didn't.

2. Do you enjoy parties?
   a. Yes, I do. b. Can I come? c. We won't.

3. Why are you leaving?
   a. No, not now. b. Because we finished our business. c. Yes, we are.

4. Where did you go on your vacation?
   a. No, I didn't. b. Yes, we went. c. To Hawaii.

5. Did you go to Europe?
   a. We went. b. No, we didn't. c. To Europe.

▶ *Write a "wh" question.*

1. You think: *(Is she going away?)*

   You ask: Where _____ ?

2. You think: *(Does he travel a lot?)*

   You ask: How often _____ ?

3. You think: *(Does he like New York?)*

   You ask: Why _____ ?

4. You think: *(Is she going alone?)*

   You ask: Who _____ ?

5. You think: *(Does she take the express train to work?)*

   You ask: Which _____ ?

How About You?

Asking questions shows you are interested in the person.
But, be careful about the type of question. In some countries,
asking personal information is rude.

▶ *Read the questions and decide: Is this type of question polite
in your country? Is it polite in the U.S.? Circle your answers.
Discuss the results with your classmates.*

Question:	Polite in your country?		Polite in the U.S.?	
1. How old are you?	Yes	No	Yes	No
2. How much did you pay for that?	Yes	No	Yes	No
3. How much do you weigh?	Yes	No	Yes	No
4. What's your salary?	Yes	No	Yes	No
5. What did you pay for your house?	Yes	No	Yes	No
6. Are you married?	Yes	No	Yes	No
7. Why aren't you married?	Yes	No	Yes	No
8. How old is your husband or wife?	Yes	No	Yes	No
9. How many children do you have?	Yes	No	Yes	No
10. Do you like your job?	Yes	No	Yes	No

It is good to be thorough in business. It is also good to be concise. Combining ideas in one sentence can make a conversation more concise.

> What does she do?
>
> She's a secretary.
> She works in the Purchasing Department.
>
> What does she do?
> She's a secretary in the Purchasing Department.

To be concise, one word can stand for a whole department.

> She's a secretary in the Personnel Department.
> She's a secretary in Personnel.

▶ *Rewrite these sentences. Make them more concise.*

1. He's an assistant in the Personnel Department.

   _____

2. She's the Vice-President of the Sales and Marketing Department.

   _____

3. He's the Assistant Manager in the Domestic Sales Department.

   _____

4. She's the Manager in the International Sales Department.

   _____

5. He's an accountant in the Accounting Department.

   _____

▶ *Combine these sentences. Write one sentence that is as concise as possible.*

1. She's a clerk in Purchasing. She works at Dale Lumber Company.

   _____

2. He's a salesman in the Pacific Rim Division. He works at Apple Computer Company.

   _____

3. She's the Manager of Domestic Sales. She works at Ford Motors.

_____

4. He's a secretary in Personnel. He works at Lockheed Aircraft.

_____

5. She's the Vice-President of Administration. She works at Acme Steel.

_____

Speak for Yourself

▶ *Work with two classmates. One of you is Speaker A; the other two are Speaker B and Speaker C. Speaker A introduces Speaker B to Speaker C. Use your real names.*

Positions:

Manager of Sales
Personnel Director
President
Assistant Manager
Administrative Assistant

Departments:

International Sales Department
Personnel Department
Accounting Department
Shipping Department
Sales and Marketing Department

Speaker A: _____, I'd like you to meet _____. _____, this is
                  Name B   Name C   Name C
           _____.
            Name B

Speaker B: How do you do, _____?
                             Name C

Speaker C: How do you do, _____? It's nice to meet you.
                             Name B

Speaker A: _____ is the _____ of _____.
            Name B   position   department

Speaker B: What do you do?

Speaker C: I'm the _____.
               position

Speaker B: I'm sorry. What do you do?

Speaker C: I'm the _____.
               position

▶ *Continue with other options; switch the roles of Speakers A, B, and C.*

▶ *Read the index in this newspaper:*

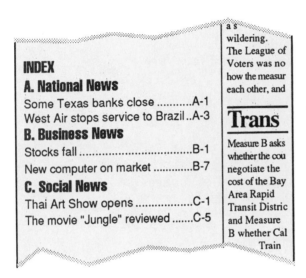

INDEX

A. National News

Some Texas banks close A-1

West Air stops service to Brazil..A-3

B. Business News

Stocks fall B-1

New computer on market B-7

C. Social News

Thai Art Show opens C-1

The movie "Jungle" reviewed C-5

a s
wildering.
The League of
Voters was no
how the measur
each other, and

Trans

Measure B asks
whether the cou
negotiate the
cost of the Bay
Area Rapid
Transit Distric
and Measure
B whether Cal
Train

▶ *Which articles might interest these people? What page should they look at? Circle your answer.*

1. Mrs. Smith collects oriental art.   A-1   C-1

2. Mr. Weiss has a ticket to Brazil on West Air.   A-3   B-7

3. Mr. Jones saw "Jungle" last night.   B-1   C-5

4. Mrs. Peters is from Texas.   A-1   B-1

5. Ms. Carey wants to sell some stock.   C-5   B-1

▶ *Look at your own newspaper. Do you see any news that might interest your own friends? Write the items and the page numbers below.*

1. _____

2. _____

3. _____

4. _____

5. _____

6. _____

A follow-up note to new clients will show them you are thinking about them. Say something about your common interests.

Situation: Mrs. Fran Shankman is interested in American art. Ms. Mary McDonald sends her an article from the newspaper.

AMERICAN ART

There is a new show of American art at the Capital City Museum...Stuart, Georgia O'Keefe, Grandma Moses, Frank Stella, Andy Warhol, and many others too numerous to me are represented in this eclectic sampl

From the desk of Mary McDonald

Fran
I saw this article on American art. I thought it would interest you.
Mary

Follow-up Note 1

Situation: Mr. Tim Worthy wants to learn how to use computers. Mr. Bernard Frank sees an announcement and sends it to him.

▶ *Fill in the blanks with one of the following words:*

    announcement   I   interest   thought

FRIDAY
Classes and Meetings
"How to Use Your Computer"
4 Hour class, 8/17 Los Angeles
Development Services: 800-395-684

From the desk of Bernard Frank

Tim,
_____saw this_____
on computers. I _____
it would _____ you.
            Bernie

Follow-up Note 2

Situation: Mr. Jack Lance likes to play golf. Mrs. Rita Reston sends him a brochure on golfing in Scotland.

▶ *Fill in the blanks with one of the following words:*

brochure   golfing   it   saw   you

St. Andrews today or Turnberry?
Golfing in Scotland

From the desk of Rita Reston

Jack,

I _____ this _____ on _____ in Scotland. I thought _____ would interest _____ .

Rita

Putting It All Together

Asking for Personal Information

▶ *Practice asking for personal information. Practice being friendly. Practice finding common interests.*

People Bingo

▶ *Use the form below to play People Bingo.*

1. Sign your name in the FREE box.
2. Walk around the room and ask: "Do you speak more than two languages?" "Do you play tennis?" Try to find out about topics first: "Who likes sports?" Then ask, "Do you play golf?"
   Have people sign their names in boxes that describe them.
3. When you fill a line of the card with signatures, shout, "Bingo!"

speaks more than 2 languages	works at night	has a dog	has lived in another country	takes the bus
has a computer	plays tennis	educated in Asia	lives more than 2 miles from school	knows someone famous
knows another alphabet	has a CD	FREE	drives a red car	is a supervisor
is an accountant	is married	plays golf	likes American food	has a VCR
has a TV	plays the piano	is single	has a roommate	reads English books for fun

▸*Make your own card and play again.*

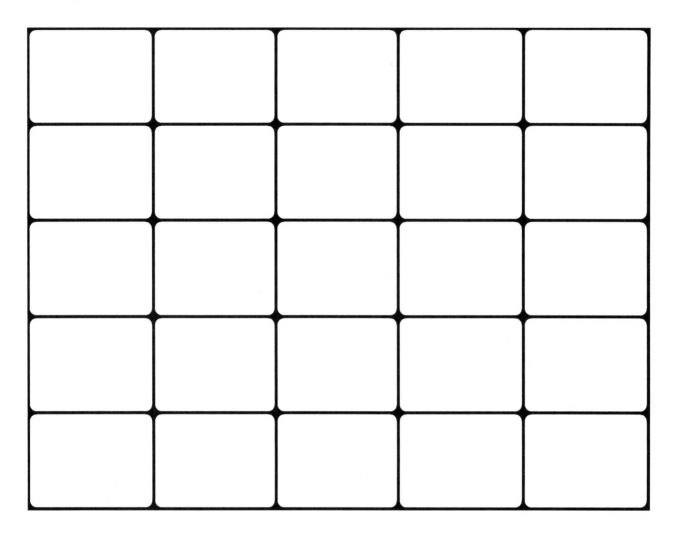

Step 4 Summary

- Use personal information in introductions.
- Whenever you meet someone, try to find a common interest.
- Write personal notes.
- Stay in touch.

Be Organized

Case Studies

Being Disorganized
Making an Appointment and Setting an Agenda

Personal Success Skills

Keeping a Calendar
Suggesting Alternatives
Being Concise

Language Skills

Using Time Expressions
Reading a Timeline
Writing "To Do" Lists

Personal Success Hint

I can't make it this afternoon, Ray. How about tomorrow morning at 10 o'clock?

Always know your schedule. If you control your time, you control your life.

Words to Know

agenda
appointment
(to) control
free time

schedule
staff meeting
timeline

Situation: Sharon Kurn wants to make a lunch appointment with Mark Stevens.

Business Idioms and Common Expressions

(to) be free for lunch	= (to) be available to have lunch
(to) run late	= (to) be behind schedule; to last longer than expected

▶ *Circle your answer.*

1. Ms. Kurn is free for lunch today.	Yes	No	Maybe
2. Mr. Stevens is free for lunch tomorrow.	Yes	No	Maybe
3. Mr. Stevens has an appointment today.	Yes	No	Maybe
4. Mr. Stevens wants to have lunch with Ms. Kurn.	Yes	No	Maybe
5. Ms. Kurn knows her schedule.	Yes	No	Maybe
6. Mr. Stevens is organized.	Yes	No	Maybe
7. Mr. Stevens is always running late.	Yes	No	Maybe

How About You?

▶ *Are you organized? Circle your answer.*

1. Is your closet neat?	Always	Sometimes	Never
2. Is your desk neat?	Always	Sometimes	Never
3. Is your address book in order?	Always	Sometimes	Never
4. Can you always find things?	Always	Sometimes	Never
5. Are you early for appointments?	Always	Sometimes	Never
6. Do you get up at the same time every day?	Always	Sometimes	Never
7. Do you plan ahead?	Always	Sometimes	Never
8. Do you make lists of things to do?	Always	Sometimes	Never

Situation: David Dasher wants to make an appointment with Nancy Gordon.

Business Idioms and Common Expressions

marketing strategy = plan for selling a product
(to) work out   = (to) develop, (to) plan
a full agenda   = a lot to do

▶ *Circle your answer.*

1. Does Mr. Dasher know his schedule?	Yes	No	Maybe
2. Does Ms. Gordon know her schedule?	Yes	No	Maybe
3. Will they meet in Ms. Gordon's office?	Yes	No	Maybe
4. Will the meeting last all day?	Yes	No	Maybe
5. Is the agenda full?	Yes	No	Maybe
6. Is Mr. Dasher organized?	Yes	No	Maybe
7. Is Ms. Gordon organized?	Yes	No	Maybe
8. Are they successful?	Yes	No	Maybe

Compare and Discuss

▶ *Compare the case studies.*

1. Why is Mr. Stevens not sure about his schedule?
2. How could Mr. Stevens become more organized?
3. What is the difference between Mark Stevens (Case Study 1) and Nancy Gordon (Case Study 2)?
4. Which person are you like—Mr. Dasher or Mr. Stevens?

Be Organized **57**

Business Abbreviations

appt = appointment
ASAP = as soon as possible
brkfst = breakfast
Co = company
dept = department
Mgr = Manager
mtg = meeting
re: = reference (about)
VP = Vice-President
w/ = with

▶ *Look at Sharon Kurn's schedule on page 59. Use the schedule to answer the questions. Put a check in the box or circle your answer.*

1. Which activities are personal and which are professional?

	Professional	Personal
Breakfast meeting	☐	☐
Tennis game	☐	☐
Telephone appointment	☐	☐
Meeting with Vice President	☐	☐

2. How many breakfast meetings are scheduled?
   a. Three   b. Two

3. When does Sharon Kurn play tennis?
   a. At 6:00 a.m.   b. At 6:00 p.m.

4. When is her free time in the afternoon?
   a. From 1:00 to 1:30   b. From 3:30 to 5:30

5. When is her free time in the morning?
   a. From 6:00 to 7:30   b. From 10:30 to 12:00

6. How long is her 1:00 p.m. meeting on August 18th?
   a. One hour   b. One and a half hours

7. What is she doing at 6:00 p.m. on August 20th?
   a. Playing golf   b. Playing tennis

8. When is her lunch appointment?
   a. On August 21   b. On August 18

9. When is the office reception?
   a. On August 19 at 7:30   b. At 8:00 on August 19

	Monday August 18	Tuesday August 19	Wednesday August 20	Thursday August 21	Friday August 22
6:00	Tennis	Tennis		Tennis	
6:30					
7:00					
7:30	Brkfst mtg		Brkfst mtg		
8:00					Haircut
8:30					
9:00	Staff mtg		mtg w/personnel		
9:30	↓	Telephone appt w/Smith re: budget			
10:00	↓				
10:30					
11:00					
11:30					
12:00				lunch w/ T. Crow	
12:30					lunch w/ B. Madden
1:00	mtg w/VP		mtg w/ accounting		
1:30	↓				
2:00			meet w/mtg planners		
2:30	mtg w/sales	Presentation for World Bank			
3:00		↓			
3:30					
4:00					
4:30					
5:00					
5:30					
6:00			Golf lesson		
6:30					
7:00	Dinner party				
7:30					
8:00		Office reception			Dinner at Waltons'

How About You?

▶ *Do you know your schedule? Write out your schedule for the coming week. First write the dates; then write the activities. Use the schedule form on page 61.*

▶ *Use your schedule to answer the questions.*

1. How much time are you in class each week?   Number of hours _____

2. How much time do you spend eating?   Number of hours _____

3. How much time do you spend studying?   Number of hours _____

4. How much free time do you have each week?   Number of hours _____

5. How much personal time do you have each week?   Number of hours _____

6. How much of your time is professional?   Number of hours _____

7. Is your schedule tight or open?   Tight   Open

Business Hint

When you make an appointment, add extra time to the appointment. For example, if someone wants to meet for 30 minutes, plan for 45 minutes on your calendar. Then if the meeting lasts 40 minutes, you are still on schedule.

Keep free time on your calendar. If you have free time, you can manage surprises. An "open" schedule is more flexible than a "tight" schedule.

	Monday	Tuesday	Wednesday	Thursday	Friday
6:00					
6:30					
7:00					
7:30					
8:00					
8:30					
9:00					
9:30					
10:00					
10:30					
11:00					
11:30					
12:00					
12:30					
1:00					
1:30					
2:00					
2:30					
3:00					
3:30					
4:00					
4:30					
5:00					
5:30					
6:00					
6:30					
7:00					
7:30					
8:00					

An organized person has plans for all possibilities. Be prepared to suggest an alternative.

▶ *Look at the model:*

Speaker A: Let's meet **tomorrow.**

Speaker B: Are you free **for lunch**?

Speaker A: No, I'm not. How about **2:30**?

Speaker B: **2:30** is fine.

▶ *Practice with your classmates.*

| Speaker A: | Let's meet | tomorrow.
next week.
Tuesday.
this afternoon. | Are you free for | lunch
dinner | at | 12:00?
7:00 a.m.?
6:00 p.m.? |

| Speaker B: | No, I'm not. How about | 1:30?
3:30?
8:00 a.m.? |

| Speaker A: | 1:30
3:30
8:00 a.m. | is fine. |

▶ *Look at this sentence.*

	(on + day)	(at + hour)	(in + time of day)
Let's meet	on Thursday on Monday on Friday	at 2:00 at 9:30 at 5:30	in the afternoon. in the morning. in the evening.

▶ *Fill in the blanks with the correct word:*

on   at   in

1. I have an appointment _____ 10:00.

2. We'll get together _____ Friday.

3. The meeting is scheduled _____ the morning.

4. There is a reception _____ the evening.

5. The office closes _____ 5:30.

▶ *Write your answer to the following questions.*

1. What time do you wake up? _____

2. What day of the week are you off? _____

3. Do you study better in the morning, in the afternoon or in the evening? _____

4. When did you eat breakfast? _____

Business Idioms and Common Expressions

to be off = not have to go to work
I'm off on Saturday and Sunday.

to go in = to go to work
I have to go in this Saturday.

Personal Success Skill Being Concise

In the business world, everyone is very busy. Business calls
are concise and "to the point." Remember to be positive.

▶ *Which is the best expression? Circle your answer.*

Situation: Mel Jones is calling to talk about his company.

1. Which of these is a good way to say "Hello"?
   a. Hello. This is Mel Jones from IMT.
   b. Hi! Guess who?

2. Which of these is "to the point"?
   a. Are you familiar with IMT and its telephone services?
   b. I'll bet you're wondering why I called.

3. Which of these is a good way to end the call?
   a. Don't hang up yet! Just one more thing.
   b. I'll call you when you have more time.

Situation: Vicky Todd is inviting a client to lunch.

1. Which of these is a good way to say "Hello"?
   a. Hello. This is Vicky Todd from Security Services.
   b. Hi! What's new?

2. Which of these is "to the point"?
   a. Are you free for lunch tomorrow?
   b. Guess what I want to do?

3. Which of these is a good way to end the call?
   a. If you have any questions, you can call me during office hours.
   b. Got to go. Call you later. Bye-bye.

Situation: Greg Thompson wants to apply for a job.

1. Which of these is a good way to say "Hello"?
   a. Ummm. Do you have any jobs?
   b. This is Greg Thompson. May I speak to the Personnel Department, please?

2. Which of these is "to the point"?
   a. Do you have any sales positions open?
   b. I was wondering if you had a job for me.

3. Which of these is a good way to end the call?
   a. Thank you for your time. I'll send my resume to your attention.
   b. If I can't find another job, I'll call you again.

Speak for Yourself

▶ *Practice with your classmates. One of you is Speaker A; the other is Speaker B.*

Situation: You are negotiating for an appointment.

Speaker A

▶ *Call a client on the phone. Try to make an appointment. Use your daily schedule on page 61 to find a free hour.*

Speaker A: Hello, _____? This is
                            name
            _____. How are you?
                  name

Speaker B:

Speaker B

▶*You are very, very busy. Try to find a time to meet with Speaker A. Use your daily schedule on page 61 to find a free hour.*

Speaker A:

Speaker B: Fine, _____. How are
                            name
            you today?

Speaker A: Great, thanks. Listen, I know you are busy now. Can we get together next week?

Speaker B:

Speaker A: How about _____?
            day

Speaker B:

Speaker A: Then how about _____?
            alternate day
(Continue until a convenient day is found.)

Speaker B:

Speaker A: How about _____?
            time

Speaker B:

Speaker A: Then how about _____?
            alternate time
(Continue until a convenient time is found.)

Speaker B:

Speaker A: Great. I'll see you on _____
                                    day
            at _____ at your office.
                time
            Have a good day.

Speaker A:

Speaker B: Sure. What day?

Speaker A:

Speaker B: *(Consult daily schedule. If the day is good, say, "OK." If not say, "That day is not good for me.")*

Speaker A:

Speaker B: *(Consult daily schedule. If the day is good, say, "OK." If not, say, "That day is not good for me.")*

Speaker A:

Speaker B: *(Consult daily schedule. If the time is good, say, "OK." If not, say, "That time is not good for me.")*

Speaker A:

Speaker B: *(Consult daily schedule. If the time is good, say, "OK." If not, say, "That time is not good for me.")*

Speaker A:

Speaker B: You, too. Bye.

▶*Continue to practice with the schedule; switch the roles of Speakers A and B.*

A timeline shows when parts of a project will be completed.

Software Development Project	
July	Meet with clients
August	Develop a proposal
September	Negotiate a contract
October	Sign the contract Start development
November-December	Test software: Version 0.5
January	Develop the packaging Develop the marketing plan Review the software design
February	Test software: Version 0.9
March	Release software: Version 1.0

▶ *Circle your answer.*

1. From start to finish, how long was the project?
   a. 9 months   b. 12 months

2. Which of these comes first?
   a. Negotiate a contract   b. Sign the contract.

3. How many months does it take to test Version 0.5?
   a. 2   b. 1

4. When is the software design reviewed?
   a. August   b. January

5. Which version is the final one?
   a. Version 1.0   Version 0.9

▶ *Rewrite the timeline.*

1. The project is delayed. It will start in September, not July.

   _____ Meet with clients
   _____ Develop a proposal
   _____ Negotiate a contract
   _____ Sign the contract
                    Start development
   _____ Test software: Version 0.5
   _____ Develop packaging
                    Develop marketing plan
                    Review software design
   _____ Test software: Version 0.9
   _____ Release software: Version 1.0

2. The project is delayed again. It will start in January. Use abbreviations for the months.

_____	Meet with clients
_____	Develop a proposal
_____	Negotiate a contract
_____	Sign the contract
	Start development
_____	Test software: Version 0.5
_____	Develop packaging
	Develop marketing plan
	Review software design
_____	Test software: Version 0.9
	Release software: Version 1.0

Abbreviations for the Months

January	Jan.
February	Feb.
March	Mar.
April	Apr.
May	May
June	June
July	July
August	Aug.
September	Sept.
October	Oct.
November	Nov.
December	Dec.

Language Skill — Writing "To Do" Lists

People who make lists are often more successful than people who don't make lists.

Today

Practice the piano
Go shopping
Finish novel

In five years

Have my own home
Speak English, Chinese, and Arabic
Learn to play the piano

▶*Write the lists for the following topics. Use another sheet of paper.*

1. Movies I want to see . . .
2. Books I want to read . . .
3. People I want to write to . . .
4. People I want to telephone . . .
5. People I want to have over for dinner . . .
6. Today I will . . .
7. This week I will . . .
8. This month I will . . .
9. This year I will . . .
10. In five years I will . . .

Putting It All Together

Working Together

Your office is moving. Your group has to decide what you are going to do first, second, third, etc. to prepare for the move. Each group will report to the class. What did your group include or leave out?

Giving Personal Information

On a piece of paper, write six sentences that list your daily activities. Tape or pin the words to your shirt or blouse. Walk around the room and read one another's list. Find out who does the same things as you—either at the same time or at different times.

Step 5 Summary

- Make appointments.
- Set agendas.
- Keep a calendar.
- Keep an open schedule.
- Be direct.
- Plan for changes.
- Be prepared with alternatives.
- Write "to do" lists.

Be Punctual

Case Studies

Arriving Late for an Appointment
Arriving Early for an Appointment

Personal Success Skills

Arriving Ahead of Schedule
Apologizing for Being Late
Accepting Apologies

Language Skills

Using the Past Tense
Reading Invitations
Writing an Apology

Personal Success Hint

I'll give him one more minute, and then I'm leaving.

When you keep someone waiting you imply, "My time is more important than yours." If you're going to be late, call and reschedule.

Words to Know

(to) apologize	latecomer
apology	on time
appointment	patient
excuse	products
fault	(to) reschedule
(to) forgive	spouse
forgiving	

Situation: Paul Ward is making a sales call on Roy Minor, the head of Purchasing. Mr. Ward wants to demonstrate his new computer products to Mr. Minor.

▶*Circle your answer.*

1. Paul Ward came to see Roy Minor.	Yes	No	Maybe
2. The appointment was for 3:00 p.m.	Yes	No	Maybe
3. Mr. Ward is running late.	Yes	No	Maybe
4. Mr. Minor is patient.	Yes	No	Maybe
5. Mr. Ward is on time.	Yes	No	Maybe
6. Mr. Ward is a salesman.	Yes	No	Maybe
7. Mr. Minor is a potential customer.	Yes	No	Maybe
8. Mr. Ward will sell Mr. Minor his computers.	Yes	No	Maybe
9. Mr. Ward is successful.	Yes	No	Maybe
10. The meeting is over at 4:45.	Yes	No	Maybe

How About You?

▶*Use these adverbs to answer the questions.*

   always   usually   sometimes   never

1. Are you punctual? _____

2. Are you on time for your teacher? _____

3. Are you on time for your supervisor? _____

4. Are you on time for dinner with your boss? _____

5. Are you late for a train departure? _____

6. Are you late for a meeting with your children's teacher? _____

7. Are you on time for a meeting with your boss? _____

Situation: Pam Green has a 2:00 appointment with Harry King. Mr. King arrives at Ms. Green's office at 1:50. She comes out to meet him at 2:00 p.m.

Business Idioms and Common Expressions

Right on time   = Not late

▶ *Circle your answer.*

1. Mr. King and Ms. Green have an appointment.	Yes	No	Maybe
2. Mr. King is punctual.	Yes	No	Maybe
3. Ms. Green is punctual.	Yes	No	Maybe
4. Ms. Green must apologize.	Yes	No	Maybe
5. Ms. Green's feelings about Mr. King are positive.	Yes	No	Maybe

Compare and Discuss

▶ *Compare the case studies.*

1. Who is more successful—Mr. King or Mr. Ward?
2. Who is more impressed—Mr. Minor or Ms. Green?
3. Whose time is more important—Mr. Minor's or Mr. Ward's?
4. What should Mr. Ward do after the meeting?
5. What should Mr. Ward do before the next meeting?
6. Are you more like Mr. King or Mr. Ward?

Business Hint

If it takes 20 minutes to go from your office to your appointment, you should leave 30 minutes before your appointment. Add extra time in case there is some problem. It is better to wait for a client than to keep a client waiting.

▶ *Look at this agenda:*

Situation: Your colleagues are making a presentation to a potential client.

```
Staff Presentation for World Bank Officials
October 16, 1997

1:00   Welcome, Jack Wilson, President
1:15   Mark Stedman, Personnel
2:00   Bill Robinson, Accounting
2:45   Jane Foresman, Administration

3:30   Coffee Break

3:45   Art Banneck, Payroll
4:30   Cynthia Wood, Marketing
5:15   Jim Reid, Management
6:00   Greg Harrison, Vice-President

6:45   Cocktail Reception
```

▶ *Circle your answer.*

1. Is Bill Robinson speaking before Ms. Foresman?	Yes	No
2. What time should Bill Robinson arrive?	1:45	2:00
3. How long is the coffee break?	One-half hour	15 minutes
4. Who is the last speaker?	Reception	Harrison
5. How many presentations are there?	Eight	Ten

▶ *Talk about the questions with your classmates.*

1. If Mark Stedman is late and starts at 1:30, what will happen?
2. If everybody takes a 25-minute coffee break, what will happen?
3. Why should everybody be on time?
4. Write the times the speakers should arrive:

Jack Wilson _____   Art Banneck _____

Mark Stedman _____   Cynthia Wood _____

Bill Robinson _____   Jim Reid _____

Jane Foresman _____   Greg Harrison _____

Sometimes you are late. If you are late, apologize. Say you
are sorry and give an excuse.

▶ *Look at the model.*

Situation: Ann Downs is George Arno's boss.

Ann Downs: You're ten minutes late.

George Arno: I'm sorry. The elevator was out of order. I had to walk up 12 flights.

▶ *Practice apologizing and giving excuses with your classmate.*

Speaker A: You're | ten minutes
half an hour   late.
one hour

Speaker B: I'm sorry. | The bus broke down.
The plane was cancelled.
The train was late.
There was an accident on the freeway.

There are two kinds of reasons for being late:

reasons within your control = YOUR fault
reasons outside your control = NOT your fault

The only excuse for being late for a business appointment is
something outside of your control. "The bus broke down."
"The subway was on strike."

I couldn't find the room.   YOUR fault
The plane was cancelled.   NOT your fault

▶ *Which of these reasons for being late are your fault? Circle
your answer.*

1. My alarm clock was broken.	Yes	No	Maybe
2. It was raining.	Yes	No	Maybe
3. The bus broke down.	Yes	No	Maybe
4. I forgot what time it was.	Yes	No	Maybe
5. My watch stopped.	Yes	No	Maybe
6. My watch is slow.	Yes	No	Maybe
7. I lost the address.	Yes	No	Maybe
8. I missed my train.	Yes	No	Maybe
9. I couldn't find a taxi.	Yes	No	Maybe
10. I overslept.	Yes	No	Maybe

When someone is late, you become worried about that person. At the same time you are often angry at that person.

When someone tells you he or she will be late, you are usually more patient. You will forgive the person for being late.

▶ *Look at the model.*

Situation: A is B's boss. B is calling from his car phone.

Business Hint

In a business situation, you should always accept an apology graciously.

Speaker A: Where are you! The meeting starts in 10 minutes!

Speaker B: I'm in my car. There's an accident on the freeway. I'm sorry I'll be late. I'll be there as soon as I can.

Speaker A: Don't worry about it. We'll start the meeting without you. Thanks for calling.

▶ *Look at these ways to accept (or not accept) an apology. Circle the type of response.*

"I'm sorry I'm late."

1. That's all right.	Patient/Forgiving	Angry/Worried
2. I was worried about you!	Patient/Forgiving	Angry/Worried
3. No problem.	Patient/Forgiving	Angry/Worried
4. Don't worry about it.	Patient/Forgiving	Angry/Worried
5. I've been here for 30 minutes.	Patient/Forgiving	Angry/Worried
6. It can happen to anyone.	Patient/Forgiving	Angry/Worried
7. You should have called!	Patient/Forgiving	Angry/Worried
8. Don't let it happen again!	Patient/Forgiving	Angry/Worried
9. Where have YOU been!	Patient/Forgiving	Angry/Worried
10. Next time call!	Patient/Forgiving	Angry/Worried

How About You?

▶ *Someone keeps you waiting for 30 minutes. What do you say? Circle your response.*

1. Your teacher says, "I'm sorry I'm late."	No problem.	Where have YOU been!
2. Your sister says, "I'm sorry I'm late."	No problem.	Where have YOU been!
3. Your father says, "I'm sorry I'm late."	No problem.	Where have YOU been!
4. Your boss says, "I'm sorry I'm late."	No problem.	Where have YOU been!
5. Your colleague says, "I'm sorry I'm late."	No problem.	Where have YOU been!
6. Your friend says, "I'm sorry I'm late."	No problem.	Where have YOU been!

Speak for Yourself

▶ *Work with a classmate. One of you is Speaker A; the other is Speaker B.*

▶ *Look at the model.*

Situation: B is always late. A, his boss, is angry.

Speaker A: You're ten minutes late.

Speaker B: I'm sorry. The bus broke down.

Speaker A: Don't let it happen again!

Speaker A

▶ *Choose a situation, time, and response.*

Situations

A is B's boss.
A and B are good friends. A is always late.
A wants to do business with B.

Time

10 minutes
45 minutes
2 hours

Response

Don't worry about it.
Don't let it happen again.
Next time, call.
I was worried about you.

Speaker A: You're _____
                        time
            minutes late.

Speaker B:

Speaker A: _____
                response

Speaker B

▶ *Choose an excuse.*

Excuses

I missed the train.
I forgot.
I was on the telephone.
The bus broke down.
The computer broke down.

Speaker A:

Speaker B: I'm sorry I'm late.
            _____.
                  excuse

Speaker A:

▶ *Do the conversation again with a different situation.*

You are late. You were supposed to be somewhere. Use the past tense to tell what happened.

(to) forget	I forgot . . .	I forgot	to set my alarm. to call a taxi. to write it in my calendar.
(to) lose	I lost . . .	I lost	my appointment book. my keys. my wallet.
(to) break (down)	. . . broke down.	The bus My car broke down. The train	
(to) run (late)	. . . ran late.	The train The bus ran late. My meeting	

▶ *Read the situation. Write a good excuse. Use the past tense of the verbs below.*

> to run late
> to break down
> to lose
> to forget

1. You were supposed to meet your friend for lunch at 12:30. It is 12:50. What happened?

_____

_____

2. You were supposed to be at a meeting at 2:00. It is 2:45. What happened?

_____

_____

3. You were supposed to be at a job interview at 10:00. It is 10:30. What happened?

_____

_____

4. You were supposed to meet a friend at 7:00. It is 7:40. What happened?

_____

_____

5. You were supposed to call a client at 3:00. It is 4:45. What happened?

_____

_____

Situation 1:

▶ *Read the following invitation.*

> You are cordially invited
> to a presentation
> by
> Mr. Ronald Preston
> on
> New Marketing Strategies
>
> Date: Monday, June 4
> Time: 2:00 p.m.
> Place: Conference Room, Second Floor

▶ *Answer the following questions. Circle your answer.*

1. What is the invitation for?	A presentation	A new market
2. What time does it start?	Monday	2:00 p.m.
3. What time will you arrive?	2:00 p.m.	1:45 p.m.
4. Is it OK to arrive late?	No	Yes

Situation 2

▶ *Read the invitation.*

> You are cordially invited
> to a reception
> for
> Mr. James Reynolds
>
> Date: Thursday, March 28
> Time: 6:00-8:00 p.m.
> Place: Executive Dining Room

▶ *Answer the questions. Circle your answer.*

1. What is the invitation for?	2 hours	A reception
2. What time does it start?	6:00 p.m.	8:00 p.m.
3. What time will you arrive?	5:45 p.m.	6:30 p.m.
4. Is it OK to arrive late?	No	Yes
5. What time will you leave?	7:45 p.m.	9:00 p.m.

Business Idioms and Common Expressions

I was unavoidably detained. = I was late, because I could not get away.

This is a polite and very common excuse.

▶ *Read the model.*

Situation: Joan Hughes arrived very late at Mr. Preston's presentation. She apologized to Mr. Preston in a short note.

From the desk of Joan Hughes

Dear Mr. Preston,

    I am very sorry I arrived late for your presentation.
I was unavoidably detained. Again, my sincere apologies.

        Sincerely yours,

        Joan Hughes

Situation 1: Max Wood arrived very late at Mr. Gray's seminar.

▶ *Apologize in a note to **Mr. Gray**. Choose from the words below:*

am   sincere
detained   yours
late

```
Dear Mr. Gray,

     I_____very sorry I arrived_____

for your presentation.  I was unavoidably _____ .

Again my _____ apologies.

               Sincerely _____,

                    Max Wood
```

Situation 2: You arrived very late at the reception for Mr. Reynolds.

▶ *Apologize in a note to **Mr. Reynolds**. Choose from the words below:*

apologies   sorry
reception   unavoidably
Sincerely

```
Dear Mr. Reynolds,

     I am very_____ I arrived late for

your _____ .  I was _____

detained.  Again my sincere _____ .


               _____ yours,


               _____
```

Putting It All Together

The 15-Second Monologue

In a small group, select one person as the time keeper. The others in your group must talk for 15-seconds—but ONLY for 15 seconds. Practice being concise.

When a person stops talking the next speaker must be ready! Before you begin, make an agenda:

AGENDA

Time	Speaker's Name	Topic		Example Topics:
00:00	_____	_____		My Favorite Book
00:15	_____	_____		My Favorite Movie
				My Favorite TV Show
00:30	_____	_____		My Weekly Schedule
00:45	_____	_____		My Morning Routine
				My Evening Routine
01:00	_____	_____		

No Excuse

Have a contest to see who can come up with the best excuse for being late. The class is divided into three teams. Two teams will compete; the third team will judge whose excuses are the best. (Rotate the teams so everyone gets to play.)

Each team creates 3-8 situations: Decide who is involved, where, and how late.

Example situations:

1. I am your boss. We had a staff meeting at 3:00 p.m. You are 20 minutes late.
2. I am your colleague. We were going to go to dinner after work. I waited at the restaurant. You never came.
3. I am your client. We were to meet on a street corner at 5:00. It is now 5:20 and it is raining. I do not have an umbrella. You are late.

Step 6 Summary

- Leave early to be sure you're not late.
- Allow extra time.
- Call to reschedule.
- Apologize if you're late.
- Accept apologies from other people.

Be Prepared

Case Studies

Giving an Unprepared Presentation
Giving a Prepared Presentation

Personal Success Skills

Being Prepared
Giving Sufficient Details
Asking the Right Questions

Language Skills

Reading Graphs and Charts
Proofreading Carefully
Recognizing Infinitives
Reading for Details
Writing with Details

Personal Success Hint

We need to prepare for tomorrow's meeting. Let's review the file.

When you meet a client or make a presentation, be prepared to state the problem, give a plan, and support the plan with details.

Words to Know

budget	digit
competition	(to) increase
(to) decrease	proposal
detail	(to) recommend
(to) develop	(to) reduce

Situation: Anne Parker has an idea for a new product. She is presenting her proposal to Karen Maple, her supervisor.

▶ *Circle your answer.*

1. Ms. Parker has an idea.	Yes	No	Maybe
2. Ms. Parker is Ms. Maple's supervisor.	Yes	No	Maybe
3. The product will take more than a year to develop.	Yes	No	Maybe
4. The new product will cost a million dollars.	Yes	No	Maybe
5. Ms. Maple asked good questions.	Yes	No	Maybe
6. Ms. Parker has done a thorough job.	Yes	No	Maybe

How About You?

▶ *Use these adverbs to tell about yourself.*

   Always   Usually   Sometimes   Never

1. Before you seal a letter, you reread the letter for errors. _____
2. Before you mail a letter, you check the address on the envelope. _____
3. You add up your check in a restaurant before paying the bill. _____
4. You keep all of your credit card receipts. _____
5. You practice your ideas on others before presenting them to an audience. _____

▶ *Discuss your answers with your classmates.*

1. What did you have for breakfast or lunch? Why? Give a short talk on the reasons you chose what you did.
2. What do you consider when you . . .
   a. choose an English book to study from?
   b. choose a movie to see?
   c. pick a company to work for?
   d. pick a vacation spot?
   e. pick a spouse?
   Why?

Situation: Martha Reynolds is a sales manager. She has a plan to increase sales. Larry Spitz is her boss.

▶ *Circle your answer.*

1. The advertising budget is too small.	Yes	No	Maybe
2. The budget was less last year.	Yes	No	Maybe
3. They spent more on print advertising than on radio.	Yes	No	Maybe
4. The competitors spent more on advertising.	Yes	No	Maybe
5. Ms. Reynolds wants to increase the advertising budget.	Yes	No	Maybe
6. Mr. Spitz asked a good question.	Yes	No	Maybe
7. Ms. Reynolds was prepared with good answers.	Yes	No	Maybe
8. They will probably increase their advertising.	Yes	No	Maybe

Compare and Discuss

▶ *Compare the case studies.*

1. Who can support her argument with facts and statistics—Ms. Parker or Ms. Reynolds?
2. Who is more impressed with their colleague—Ms. Maple or Mr. Spitz?
3. Who would you like to work with—Ms. Parker or Ms. Reynolds?
4. Why is Ms. Reynolds' presentation more interesting?

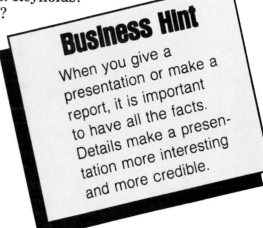

Business Hint

When you give a presentation or make a report, it is important to have all the facts. Details make a presentation more interesting and more credible.

Before you go into a meeting, be prepared. Think of the questions people will ask. Prepare answers for these questions. Know how long, how much, and what is required to do something.

Read the model:

Anne Parker: I think we should develop a new product.

Karen Maple: How long will it take **to develop**?

Anne Parker: It will take **18 months**.

Karen Maple: How much will it cost?

Anne Parker: It will cost **$4,000**.

▶ *Practice with your classmates:*

Speaker A: I think we should | develop a new product.
redo our budget.
rewrite our catalog.

Speaker B: How long will it take | to develop?
to do?
to write?

Speaker A: It will take | 18 months.
a few hours.
a week.

Speaker B: How much will it | cost?
be?
take?

Speaker A: It will | cost $4,000.
be about $1,000.
take about 2 million.

▶ *Think of other situations and do the conversation again.*

The more information you give, the less people will have to ask.

Speaker A: I had **lunch**.

Speaker B: *When* did you have lunch?

Speaker A: I had lunch **at noon**.

Speaker B: *Where* did you have lunch at noon?

Speaker A: I had lunch at noon **at the Four Seasons restaurant**.

Speaker B: *With whom* did you have lunch at noon at the Four Seasons?

Speaker A: I had lunch at noon at the Four Seasons restaurant **with my brother**.

▶ *Work with a classmate. Speaker A chooses a situation to start the conversation. Speaker B chooses "wh" questions to ask.*

Lunch Breakfast Supper Snack Meeting Class

What? When? Where? At what time? With whom? Why?

Language Skill · Reading Graphs and Charts

A pie chart is used to show percentages of a whole.

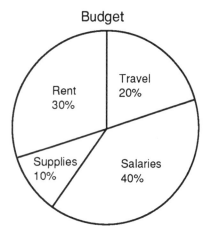

Budget

Rent 30%
Travel 20%
Supplies 10%
Salaries 40%

▶ *Answer these questions.*

1. What percentage is budgeted for travel? _____

2. What percentage is budgeted for rent? _____

3. How much more is budgeted for salaries than supplies? _____

4. Which item is the greatest percentage? _____

A line graph is used to show increases and decreases.

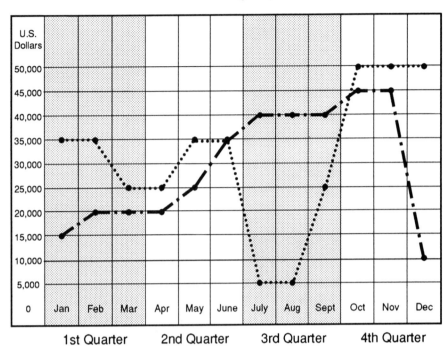

Advertising Expenses

Print   ●－·－●

TV   ●·······●

▶ *Answer these questions.*

1. How much was spent on print advertising in January? _____

2. How much was spent on print and TV advertising in March? _____

3. How much more was spent on TV than on print advertising in November?

_____

4. Which quarter was the total TV advertising $150,000? _____

5. Complete the chart.

Print Advertising	Totals	TV Advertising	Totals
1st Quarter	U.S.$55,000	1st Quarter	_____
2nd Quarter	_____	2nd Quarter	_____
3rd Quarter	_____	3rd Quarter	U.S.$35,000
4th Quarter	_____	4th Quarter	_____
Total:	_____	Total:	_____

A bar graph is also used to show combined increases and decreases.

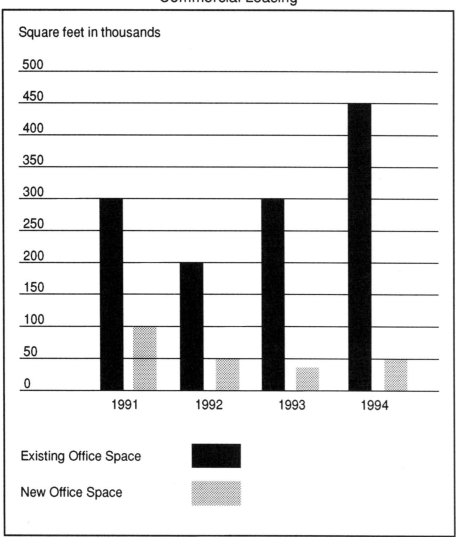

Commercial Leasing

Square feet in thousands

Existing Office Space

New Office Space

▶ *Answer these questions.*

1. How many square feet was leased all together in 1991? _____

2. How many square feet of new office space was leased in 1991? _____

3. How much space was leased all together in 1994? _____

4. How many square feet of existing office space was leased in 1994? _____

5. In what year was the least space in existing buildings leased? _____

6. In what year do you think fewer new office buildings were built? 1993 or 1994?

_____

A good manager knows how to ask the right question to get the right answer. The right question is one that gets a lot of information.

Remember a "wh" question gets more information than a yes/no question.

Speaker A: Are newspaper ads effective?

Speaker B: Yes.

Speaker A: How effective are newspaper ads?

Speaker B: We receive 3500 leads for every ad.

▶ *Look at the graphs in the last exercises. Rewrite these questions using a "wh" expression.*

1. Was new office space leased in 1991?

   How much _____

2. Was a percentage of the expenses spent on rent?

   What _____

3. Was money spent on TV advertising in the fourth quarter?

   How much _____

4. Was more money spent on advertising in the third quarter?

   In which _____

When you proofread your letters and reports, you have to be careful that there are no typos. Typos are mistakes made when typing. Note the symbols used to correct these errors.

Here are some common errors: Proofing Symbols

Leaving out a word	Leaving out a word.
Leaving out a letter	Leaving out a leter.
Reversing words	words Reversing
Reversing letters	Reversing lettres

▶ *All of the following sentences have mistakes. How many
mistakes are in the sentence? Circle your answer.*

1. There no is competition.	One	Two
2. Product will cost two million dollar.	One	Two
3. She gave thorough proposal.	One	Two
4. The new product interesting.	One	Two
5. The report givse a lot of details.	One	Two
6. I not sure how much will cost.	One	Two
7. The minutes of the meeting mathced the agenda.	One	Two

There were nine errors. How many did you find? Write the
number here: _____

▶ *Use the proofing symbols and correct the errors.*

Language Skill   Recognizing Infinitives

▶ *Look at this model:*

We need | **to get** more details.
to ask some questions.
to finish this report.

Write the correct answer.

to copy   to answer   to increase   to make

1. I need _____ the phone.   3. You need _____ a reservation.

2. Ms. Smith needs _____ the agenda.   4. They need _____ sales.

▶ *Write the answer to the question.*

1. The phone is ringing. What do you need to do?

_____

2. Sales are down. What do we need to do?

_____

3. I don't have a hotel reservation. What do I need to do?

_____

4. They don't have a copy of my report. What do I need to do?

_____

▶*Read the following announcement from the company bulletin board.*

All managers are invited to a meeting,

"How To Manage Projects"

The meeting will be in the conference room from 2:00 to 4:30 on Thursday, January 10.

Speakers: Mark Colson and Joan Appleton

Call Rick Crane at 340-7979 for more information.

▶*Find the details. Circle your answer.*

1. What is the announcement about?	A meeting	Projects
2. Who is invited?	Speakers	Managers
3. Where will the meeting be?	On Thursday	In the conference room
4. How long will the meeting be?	2 hours	2 1/2 hours
5. What is the date of the meeting?	Jan. 1	Jan. 10
6. How many speakers will there be?	Two	Three
7. Who do you call for more information?	Colson	Crane
8. Do all managers have to go?	Yes	No
9. What is Mr. Crane's telephone number?	304-9797	340-7979
10. What day is the meeting?	Tuesday	Thursday

▸*Read the model notes for an announcement. Then read the model announcement.*

Notes:

> Business Meeting
> "Starting a New Business:
> How much does it cost?"
> Friday, May 2, 2:30 p.m.,
> Carter Auditorium,
> 495 Elm Street. Free.
> Call (412) 456-6845

Announcement:

> There will be a business meeting,
>
> ## "Starting a New Business: How much does it cost?"
>
> Friday, May 2, 2:30 p.m., Carter Auditorium, 495 Elm Street. Free admission.
> Call (412) 456-6845 for more information.

Announcement 1

▸*Read the notes. Then write the announcement.*

> Notes:
> Planning Meeting
> "Marketing New
> Products," Monday,
> March 6, 4:00 p.m.,
> Fairview Hotel,
> 6940 Amherst Avenue.
> Free. Call (613) 459-6832.

> There will be a _____ meeting.
> "_____ "
> on _____, at _____ p.m.
> The meeting will be at the _____
> at _____ .
> The admission is _____ .
> Call _____ for more information.

Announcement 2

▶ *Read the notes. Then write the announcement.*

Meeting for small
Businesses
"Sales and Marketing,"
1:00 PM, July 30
(Tuesday) City View
Hotel, 960 67th Avenue.
$10.
Call 703/594-7854

There will be a meeting for businesses,

"_____ " on _____ ,

_____ at _____ PM. The

meeting will be at the _____ at

_____ . The admission is

_____ . Call _____ for

more information.

Announcement 3

▶ *Read the notes. Then write the announcement.*

**From the desk of
Bill Rodgers**

World Trade Seminar
"New Trade Policy"
Friday, Dec. 12, 3:30 p.m.
World Conference Center
Drysdale Circle. $125.
Call (512) 433-3344

_____
_____
_____
_____
_____
_____
_____
_____
_____
_____
_____

Putting It All Together

Preparing a Budget

▶*You must help plan a budget for a trip. As a class:*

1. choose a city: _____
2. a reason for going to that city: _____
3. how many people can go: _____
4. how long the trip will be: _____

▶*In small groups, decide:*

5. How much will you spend on . . .
   a. airfare: _____
   b. hotels: _____
   c. meals: _____
   d. taxis: _____
   e. tips: _____
   f. gifts: _____
6. What else will you need money for? _____

▶*Prepare a pie graph for the budget above.*

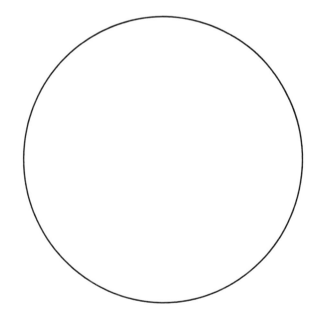

Making a Presentation

In small groups, each person picks a topic for a 30-second presentation. Plan your presentation. Announce your topic to the group. Each member writes a question s/he thinks your presentation will answer. (Ask "wh" questions to get more information.) Don't look at these questions. Give your presentation. Now read the questions. Did you answer their questions?

Possible Topics:
> How to Make a Photocopy
> Finding a Taxi
> Drawing a Graph

Writing a Note for an Announcement

Write a note with the information about your presentation. When is it? Where is it? How much does it cost? Where can they call for more information? Give your note to a classmate. Have him/her write an announcement about your presentation. Give the announcement to another classmate. Have it proofed. When it is correct, post it.

Step 7 Summary

- Be prepared.
- Give sufficient details.
- Ask the right questions.
- Proofread carefully.

Be Polite

Case Studies

Being Impolite on the Phone
Being Polite on the Phone

Personal Success Skills

Identifying Yourself
Stating Your Purpose
Using Polite Expressions
Suggesting Alternatives

Language Skills

Expressing Appreciation
Reading Telephone Messages
Writing Telephone Messages

Personal Success Hint

Thank you for your help.

You're welcome. I'll be sure to give Mr. Smith your message.

It pays to be polite in business.

Words to Know

emergency
impolite
(to) leave a message

(to) make small talk
polite
(to) take a message

Case Study

Being Impolite on the Phone

Situation: Barbara McKain is the receptionist at Green and Sons Company. One of her duties is to answer the telephone. No one gets past Ms. McKain.

►*Circle your answer.*

1. Is Mrs. Croft calling Mr. Green?	Yes	No	Maybe
2. Is Mrs. Croft polite?	Yes	No	Maybe
3. Is Mr. Green in the office?	Yes	No	Maybe
4. Is Ms. McKain polite?	Yes	No	Maybe
5. Will Mrs. Croft call back?	Yes	No	Maybe

How About You?

►*Use these adverbs to tell about yourself.*

always   usually   sometimes   never

1. I am polite to strangers when face-to-face. _____

2. I am polite to strangers when on the phone. _____

3. I am polite to acquaintances. _____

4. I am more polite to strangers than to my family. _____

Situation: Jack Winston is talking to Barbara McKain, the receptionist.

▶*Circle your answer.*

1. Is Mr. Winston calling Mr. Green?	Yes	No	Maybe
2. Did Mr. Winston have a vacation?	Yes	No	Maybe
3. Was Mr. Winston polite?	Yes	No	Maybe
4. Is Mr. Green in the office?	Yes	No	Maybe
5. Was Barbara polite?	Yes	No	Maybe
6. Will Mr. Green call Mr. Winston?	Yes	No	Maybe
7. Did Mr. Winston "get past the secretary"?	Yes	No	Maybe

Compare and Discuss

▶*Compare the case studies.*

1. Who is more polite—Mr. Winston or Mrs. Croft?
2. Why is Ms. McKain nice to Mr. Winston?
3. Why does Mr. Winston call Ms. McKain, Barbara?
4. Who is a positive person—Mr. Winston or Mrs. Croft?
5. Who is more successful—Mr. Winston or Mrs. Croft?
6. Who would you rather talk to—Mr. Winston or Mrs. Croft?
7. Do you like secretaries to ask why you are calling?

When you answer your phone at the office, you should identify yourself:

>Hello. Charles Palmer.
>
>Hello. Charles Palmer speaking.
>
>Hello. Charles Palmer here.
>
>Hello. This is Charles Palmer.

When you call someone, you should identify yourself and give your company name:

>Hello, Mr. Palmer. This is Rob Cranston from Parent Magazine.
>
>Hello, Mr. Palmer. This is Jane Doyle from IBM calling.

▶*Practice with your classmate saying "Hello" on the telephone.*

Speaker A: Hello. | (Speaker A name) speaking.
(Speaker A name) here.
This is (Speaker A name).

Speaker B: Hello, _____ This is _____ from
                         Speaker A name   Speaker B name

_____ calling.
   company

Business Idioms and Common Expressions

(to) get past the secretary = (to) talk to the secretary so that he/she will let you talk to her boss

to step out = (to) leave the office for a short time

It's none of your business. = a rude expression that means: "I'm not going to tell you. It should not interest you."

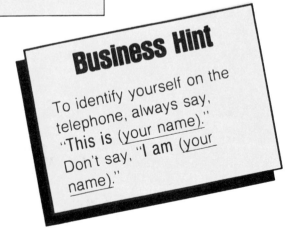

Business Hint

To identify yourself on the telephone, always say, "This is (your name)." Don't say, "I am (your name)."

Personal Success Skill — Stating Your Purpose

▸ *Read the conversations.*

A Polite Conversation:

Speaker A: May I help you?

Speaker B: Yes, please. Could I speak to Mr. Carlson?

An Impolite Conversation:

Speaker A: What do you want?

Speaker B: Mr. Carlson.

▸ *Match the polite and impolite expressions. Write the letter of the impolite expression that means the same as the polite expression.*

Polite Expressions	Impolite Expressions
___ 1. May I help you?	a. I want Mr. Fox.
___ 2. Could I speak to Mr. Fox?	b. Who is this?
___ 3. Who may I ask is calling?	c. Make it quick.
___ 4. Could you help me?	d. Jim.
___ 5. This is an emergency.	e. What do you want?
___ 6. I'd like to speak to Jim, please.	f. Get me some help.

Personal Success Skill — Using Polite Expressions

▸ *Which expression is more polite? Circle the letter.*

1. a. Where is a telephone?
   b. Could you tell me where a telephone is?
2. a. What's your fax number?
   b. Could you give me your fax number, please?
3. a. What did you say?
   b. Could you please repeat that?
4. a. It's none of your business.
   b. I'd rather not say.
5. a. What do you want?
   b. May I help you?

▶ *Practice using polite expressions.*

Speaker A:
| May
| Could | I help you?
| Can

Speaker B: Yes, please. I'd like to speak to
| Mrs. Fry.
| the secretary.
| the manager.

Speaker A:
| Of course.
| Certainly. Just a moment, please.
| Surely.

▶ *Now practice with a classmate.*

Speaker A: _____ I help you?

Speaker B: Yes, please. I'd like to speak to _____.

Speaker A: _____. Just a moment, please.

Business Idioms and Common Expressions

If you are busy doing something, you can say, "I'm in the middle
| a meeting."
of | dinner."
| a conversation."

Personal Success Skill Suggesting Alternatives

If you need to get off the phone, provide a reason and a
suggestion to continue later.

Charles Palmer: Mr. Cranston, I'm in the middle of a
                 meeting. Could we talk later?

Rob Cranston: Of course. When should I call?

Charles Palmer: Call me in about 20 minutes, please.

Reasons:

I'm in the middle of a meeting.
I'm on my way to a meeting.
I can't talk now.
I'm very busy right now.

Suggestions

Could we talk later?
Could you call me this afternoon?
Call me tomorrow, please.
Call me in about an hour, please.

▶ *Practice ending phone calls with a classmate.*

Speaker A: _____ , | Someone is in my office.
| I can't talk now.
| I'm on my way to a meeting.
| I just got in.
| I'm on my way to lunch.

Could you please call me later?

Speaker B: Of course. When should I call?

Speaker A: Call me | in about an hour.
| tomorrow morning.
| at 3:00.
| in two hours.
| early tomorrow.

Language Skill — Expressing Appreciation

▶ *Study these sentences:*

Thanks	for	asking.
Thank you		calling.
		coming.

▶ *Read the situation. What do you say?*

1. Situation: Somebody asked about your job.

   You say: Thank you for _____

2. Situation: Somebody came to your party.

   You say: _____

3. Situation: Somebody helped you.

   You say: _____

4. Situation: Somebody asked about your family.

   You say: _____

5. Situation: Somebody called you.

   You say: _____

▶ *Read the following message.*

Situation: Bob Wright called Jack Barnes. The secretary took a message.

▶ *Circle your answer.*

1. Mr. Barnes had a telephone message.	Yes	No	Maybe
2. Jack Barnes read the telephone message.	Yes	No	Maybe
3. Bob White called Jack Barnes.	Yes	No	Maybe
4. Mr. Barnes called Mr. Wright.	Yes	No	Maybe
5. Jack Barnes called Mr. White.	Yes	No	Maybe
6. Mr. Wright is annoyed.	Yes	No	Maybe
7. The secretary made a mistake.	Yes	No	Maybe
8. The secretary did not ask for clarification.	Yes	No	Maybe

Business Hint

Pronounce names and numbers slowly and clearly on the telephone. Telephone conversations are often difficult to understand. Why?

▸*Practice taking phone messages. One of you is Speaker A; the other is Speaker B. Make up new conversations after doing the first two.*

▸*Use the message forms on page 104 to record the information in the conversation.*

Speaker A

Speaker A: Good morning. May I help you?

Speaker B:

Speaker A: I'm sorry. | Mr. Robson
                      | Ms. Quinn
just stepped out. May I take a message?

Speaker B:

Speaker A: And your number
| Ms. Tracy?
| Mr. Goodman?

Speaker B:

Speaker A: Let me repeat that. _____
                                  spell

_____
name and read number

Speaker B:

Speaker A: Thank you for calling. Good-by.

Speaker B

Speaker A:

Speaker B: Yes, may I speak
to | Mr. Bill Robson?
   | Ms. Sally Quinn?

Speaker A:

Speaker B: Yes, please tell | him
                            | her
that | Mark Goodman
     | Lisa Tracy
returned | her   call.
         | his

Speaker A:

Speaker B: Area code 203-434-5504.
I'll call | him   after lunch.
          | her

Speaker A:

Speaker B: That's correct. Thank you very much.

Speaker A:

While You Were Out

Date: _____ Time: _____

Caller: _____

Telephone Number: _____

Message: _____

_____

_____

_____

_____

_____

While You Were Out

Date: _____ Time: _____

Caller: _____

Telephone Number: _____

Message: _____

_____

_____

_____

_____

_____

While You Were Out

Date: _____ Time: _____

Caller: _____

Telephone Number: _____

Message: _____

_____

_____

_____

_____

_____

While You Were Out

Date: _____ Time: _____

Caller: _____

Telephone Number: _____

Message: _____

_____

_____

_____

_____

_____

Putting It All Together

Messages

1. Have classmates leave a message on your "answering machine." Pass around a tape recorder. Each student will leave a message. You write the message down and decide when to return the call.

2. Try talking to people outside of class using both polite and impolite language. What are their reactions?

3. Write the personal success skill that matches the conversation for Speaker A.

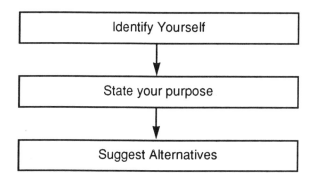

Speaker A: Hello this is John Wilson. _____
Speaker B: Yes, Mr. Wilson. How may I
help you?
Speaker A: May I speak with Mr.
Roderick? _____
Speaker B: I'm sorry he's in a meeting
now.
Speaker A: Perhaps he can call me later. _____
Speaker B: Yes. I'll tell him you called.

Role Play

Be polite even if the other person is rude. Choose a partner. You are the receptionist. Your partner wants to talk to the boss, NOW! S/he will be very rude. You must be very polite.

Small Talk

What are some appropriate topics for small talk? In a small group, make a list. Pick a topic, write it on a piece of paper, and pin it to your shirt. Walk around the room (like you would at a cocktail party) and introduce yourself to someone. Talk about the topic pinned to their shirts. Keep changing partners until you have made small talk with everyone.

Step 8 Summary

- Identify yourself on the phone.
- Speak slowly and clearly.
- Return your phone calls.
- Express appreciation.

Be Patient

Case Studies

Giving Negative Feedback
Giving Positive Feedback

Personal Success Skills

Giving Positive Suggestions
Making Positive Comments
Making Polite Requests

Language Skills

Using *This* and *There* as Subjects
Using the Passive Voice
Reading Instructions
Using *Should*
Writing Polite Requests

Personal Success Hint

Take your time to learn this new computer program. It will help you in the long run.

Good work can take time to accomplish.

Words to Know

(to) compliment	(to) retype
(to) criticize	strength
mistake	suggestion
(to) redo	weakness

Situation: Alice Duff supervises Wilma Cochran, who is a typist.

▶*Circle your answer.*

1. Is Ms. Duff a supervisor?	Yes	No	Maybe
2. Is this the first time Ms. Cochran typed a letter?	Yes	No	Maybe
3. Is Ms. Cochran a careful typist?	Yes	No	Maybe
4. Is Ms. Duff patient?	Yes	No	Maybe
5. Will Ms. Cochran retype the letter?	Yes	No	Maybe
6. Is Ms. Duff polite?	Yes	No	Maybe
7. Will Ms. Duff type the letter?	Yes	No	Maybe

How About You?

▶*Circle your answer.*

1. To do a job right, I do it myself.	Yes	No	Sometimes
2. I never make a mistake.	Yes	No	Sometimes
3. I explain things carefully.	Yes	No	Sometimes
4. I give everyone a second chance.	Yes	No	Sometimes
5. I check my work carefully.	Yes	No	Sometimes
6. I fix mistakes neatly.	Yes	No	Sometimes

Situation: Gail Brooks typed a letter for Charles Decker.

▶*Circle your answer.*

1. Was Mr. Decker negative?	Yes	No	Maybe
2. Did Mr. Decker correct Ms. Brooks?	Yes	No	Maybe
3. Was Ms. Brooks positive?	Yes	No	Maybe
4. Will Mr. Decker fix the problem?	Yes	No	Maybe
5. Will they work well together?	Yes	No	Maybe

Compare and Discuss

▶*Compare the case studies.*

1. Who is more patient—Ms. Duff or Mr. Decker?
2. Who do you want to work with—Ms. Cochran or Ms. Brooks?
3. Who do you want to work for—Ms. Duff or Mr. Decker?
4. Is making a typo a serious mistake?
5. Is forgetting the date a serious mistake?
6. Which is worse—making a typo or forgetting the date?

Business Hint

Never forget to use the words *please* and *thank you.*

Giving Positive Suggestions

When you give instructions, be patient. Explain how things
should be done.

Positive Suggestion: In this office, we use wider margins.

Polite Request: Could you retype this letter with wider margins?

▶ *Match the positive suggestion with the appropriate polite
request.*

Positive Suggestions

1. In this office, we always use white
   paper for letters.
2. In this office, we are very clean and
   organized.
3. In this office, everyone helps the
   receptionist.
4. In this office, we are always punctual.

Polite Requests

a. Could you please come on time
   tomorrow?
b. Could you please clean your desk before
   you leave?
c. Could you please answer the phone
   while she's at lunch?
d. Could you please retype your letter?

Personal Success Skill Making Positive Comments

A positive comment makes people comfortable and ready
to listen.

Negative comment: You can't do anything right!

Positive Comment: Thanks for trying. I really appreciate it.

▶ *Rewrite these sentences.*

I really appreciate your help.

Thanks for _____.

1. I really appreciate your staying late.

   _____

2. I really appreciate your meeting me.

   _____

3. I really appreciate your coming early.

   _____

4. I really appreciate your working overtime.

   _____

When there is a problem, it is better to be polite.

Impolite: Do it again and do it right!

Polite: Could you please do it again?

▶ *Study the chart.*

(to) redo	= (to) do it again
(to) retype	= (to) type again
(to) reread	= (to) read again
(to) reprint	= (to) print again
(to) rewrite	= (to) write again
(to) recopy	= (to) copy again

▶ *Rewrite the sentences. Use one word for the underlined words.*

1. Could you please print this report again? _____

2. Could you please type this again? _____

3. Could you please read this again? _____

4. Could you please do this again? _____

5. Could you please write the numbers again? _____

Language Skill

Using *This* and *There* as Subjects

A polite way to correct someone is to make the correction impersonal. Try not to use the word *you*.

Problem: You didn't type the address on the letter.

Polite Correction: There is no address on the letter.

▶ *Which is a more polite correction? Circle the letter.*

1. a: This is not the right file.
   b: You gave me the wrong file.

2. a: You gave me the wrong number.
   b: This is not the right number.

3. a: You gave me the wrong address.
   b: This is not the right address.

4. a: This is not the right envelope.
   b: You gave me the wrong envelope.

A polite way to correct someone is to use the passive voice. Rather than say "YOU made a mistake," say "A mistake was made."

> Problem: You didn't type the address on the letter.
>
> Polite Correction: The letter was addressed incorrectly.

▶ *Which is a more polite correction? Circle the letter.*

1. a: You wrote the name incorrectly.
   b: The name was written incorrectly.

2. a: You called the wrong customer.
   b: The wrong customer was called.

3. a: You sent the wrong letter.
   b: The wrong letter was sent.

4. a: You made a mistake.
   b: A mistake was made.

▶ *Look at the model.*

Situation: Speaker B didn't type the address on the letter.

> Speaker A: This letter was addressed incorrectly.
>
> Speaker B: I'm sorry. I'll *retype* it.

▶ *Practice giving corrections to your classmates. Use the following action words.*

> rewrite   call again   send again   copy again   retype

1. Speaker B wrote the wrong name.
   Speaker A:
   Speaker B:

2. Speaker B called the wrong customer.

3. Speaker B sent the wrong letter.

4. Speaker B made a bad copy.

5. Speaker B made two typos.

Business Hint

"You catch more flies with honey than with vinegar."
This common English expression means: if you are nice (sweet), people will do what you ask; if you are nasty (bitter like vinegar), people will not want to do what you ask.

▶ *Read the memo.*

Memorandum

To: All Training Personnel
From: R. Markham *RM*
         Head, Training Department
Subject: Providing Clear, Complete Instructions

It has come to my attention that new employees are
not performing their jobs satisfactorily. This is
the fault of the trainer, not the trainee. You
should give clear, complete instructions.

Please follow these guidelines:

    1. Give an overview of the task.
       Make sure the task is understood.
    2. Describe each step in order.
    3. Describe each step thoroughly.
    4. Ask questions at each step.
       Do NOT ask: Do you understand?
       Ask: How do we begin? What do we do next? etc.
    5. Have trainees repeat the instructions.

Business Hint

A notice sent to employees within a company is called a memorandum, or "memo" for short.

▶ *Circle your answer.*

1. Who wrote the memo?
   a. A trainee
   b. A trainer

2. What is the memo about?
   a. Giving instructions
   b. Hiring trainers

3. If a trainee does not understand instructions, whose fault is it?
   a. The trainee's
   b. The trainer's

4. Which should be explained first?
   a. Step 1 of the task
   b. An overview of the task.

5. Which is a better question?
   a. What's the first step?
   b. Do you understand?

To make a polite suggestion, use the word *should*.

An impolite suggestion: You had better finish your report.

A polite suggestion: You should finish your report.

▶ *Write the sentence as a polite suggestion.*

1. We ought to talk about the problem.

_____

2. He'd better know her name.

_____

3. I'd better finish the report.

_____

4. Mrs. Vernon ought to call right now.

_____

5. The manager ought to write an agenda.

_____

Language Skill   Writing Polite Requests

▶ *Study the model.*

June 19, 1919

Dear Mr. Wilson,

Thank you so much for

From the desk of Donald King

Please note the mistake on the date. Could you redo it right away? Thank you,

DK

▶*Write the words to complete the notes.*

Situation 1

April 4

Dear Mrs. greenly,

We received your order

From the desk of Mary Clark

_____ note the mistake on the _____. Could you _____ it right away?

Thank you,

_____

Situation 2

The costs are as follows:

                    15.00
                    20.00
                    35.00
Total: 60.00
Please send the total

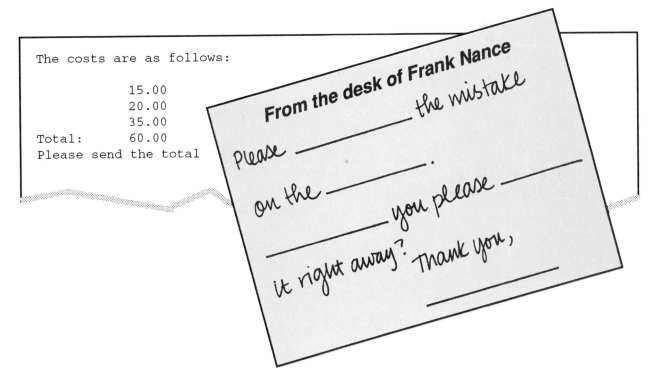

From the desk of Frank Nance

Please _____ the mistake on the _____. _____ you please _____ it right away? Thank you,

_____

Putting It All Together

Giving Feedback

1. Write the personal success skill that matches the conversation for Speaker A.

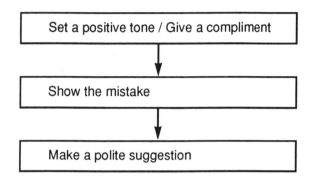

Set a positive tone / Give a compliment

Show the mistake

Make a polite suggestion

Speaker A: You did a nice job with this report. _____
Speaker B: Thanks Mr. Decker.
Speaker A: There was no date on the letter, though. _____
Speaker B: I'm sorry. I'll fix that right away.
Speaker A: Thank you. Would you please fax it then? _____
Speaker B: Right away.

2. Give your classmate a task. Ask him or her to write directions for the route to a restaurant, to write a letter for you, to write out instructions to use the telephone, etc. Can the task be improved? How? Tell your classmate what is good about his or her work and make a positive suggestion for improvement.

Step 9 Summary

- Always say *please* and *thank you*.
- Be positive.
- Compliment good work.
- Point out errors politely.
- Provide clear, complete instructions.

Be Loyal

Case Studies

Not Sharing the Credit
Sharing the Credit

Personal Success Skills

Sharing the Credit
Working Beyond Your Job Description
Sharing Responsibility

Language Skills

Using *We*, *Us*, and *Our*
Assigning Tasks
Reading a Letter of Congratulations
Writing a Thank-you Letter

Personal Success Hint

We got the Jackson order, and it's due to the efforts of everyone in this room. Thank you all!

There is an expression in English: "Give credit where credit is due." By sharing your success, you show loyalty to your colleagues, your boss, and your company.

Words to Know

(to) blame	(to be) qualified
(to) give credit	responsibility
(to) hire	(to) share
loyalty	

117

Situation: Richard Costner is Ann Edwards's boss.

Business Idioms and Common Expressions

(To) work night and day = Work long hours
Lunch break = Rest period to eat lunch
Between you and me = Don't tell anyone this.
(To) make a sale = Successfully sell a product or proposa

▶ *Circle your answer.*

1. Did Ann make the sale?	Yes	No	Maybe
2. Did Ann make the sale alone?	Yes	No	Maybe
3. Is Ann loyal to her colleagues?	Yes	No	Maybe
4. Is Ann loyal to her company?	Yes	No	Maybe
5. Is Ann loyal to her supervisor, Mr. Costner?	Yes	No	Maybe
6. Is Mr. Costner pleased with Ann?	Yes	No	Maybe
7. Will Ann be working there much longer?	Yes	No	Maybe

How About You?

▶ *Circle your answer.*

1. Do you use *we* more than *I*?	Always	Sometimes	Never
2. Do you share credit?	Always	Sometimes	Never
3. Do you share blame?	Always	Sometimes	Never
4. Are you loyal to your colleagues?	Always	Sometimes	Never
5. Are you loyal to your classmates?	Always	Sometimes	Never
6. Are you loyal to your school?	Always	Sometimes	Never
7. Are you loyal to your teacher?	Always	Sometimes	Never
8. Do you thank people who help you?	Always	Sometimes	Never

Situation: Pam King is part of Bruce Grayson's task force.

Business Idioms and Common Expressions

Team effort   = Employees work together on a project.
The credit goes to you. = You are responsible for our success.

▶ *Circle your answer.*

1. Ms. King did a great job.	Yes	No	Maybe
2. Ms. King worked alone.	Yes	No	Maybe
3. Mr. Grayson praises Ms. King's work.	Yes	No	Maybe
4. Ms. King takes all the credit.	Yes	No	Maybe
5. Pam King gives Mr. Grayson credit.	Yes	No	Maybe
6. All the credit goes to Mr. Grayson.	Yes	No	Maybe
7. Mr. Grayson is impressed with Ms. King.	Yes	No	Maybe

Compare and Discuss

▶ *Compare the case studies.*

1. Who is more loyal—Ms. Edwards or Ms. King?
2. Who is a better worker—Ms. Edwards or Ms. King?
3. Who do you want to work with—Ms. Edwards or Ms. King?
4. When is it important to share credit?
5. When is it important to share blame?
6. Who is most likely to be promoted—Ms. Edwards or Ms. King?
7. Rewrite the first case study so Ms. Edwards shares the credit.

Sharing the Credit

There is a common English expression: "The whole is greater than the sum of its parts." When people work well together, the company benefits and the individuals benefit.

▶ *Which statement expresses "Sharing the Credit"? Which expresses "Taking the Credit"? Check the appropriate box.*

	Sharing the Credit	Taking the Credit
1. I did it all myself.	☐	☐
2. I had a lot of help.	☐	☐
3. It was a team effort.	☐	☐
4. I couldn't have done it without you.	☐	☐
5. We all worked together.	☐	☐
6. No one else helped me.	☐	☐
7. Without me, it wouldn't have happened.	☐	☐
8. I must credit my colleagues.	☐	☐
9. We all did our part.	☐	☐
10. You three deserve the credit.	☐	☐

Personal Success Skill Working Beyond Your Job Description

When you work on a project as part of a team, there are many tasks that have to be done. Sometimes, these tasks are not what you were hired to do. You do them because you want to help get the project done.

▶ *Practice with your classmates. Give positive responses to these requests:*

Speaker A: Would you

send this fax?
type this memo?
finish this report?
copy these letters?
file these papers?
get us some coffee?
call the client?
make reservations at the hotel?

Speaker B:

Yes, of course.
No problem.
Right away.
Yes, I will.
I'll be happy to help.

Kings, queens, emperors, and other royalty refer to
themselves as *We*. Politicians and journalists often refer
to themselves as *we*. Using *we* shares responsibility, credit,
and blame. You should use *we* at the office.

Look at this list of pronouns.

I	me	my	myself	we	us	our	ourselves
you	you	your	yourself	you	you	your	yourselves

▶ *Change the underlined personal pronouns to* we, us *or* our.

1. I did it all <u>myself</u>. _____
2. To do a job right, let <u>me</u> do it. _____
3. <u>I</u> finished ahead of schedule. _____
4. <u>I</u> made the sale <u>myself</u>. _____
5. It was <u>my</u> report that won the client. _____

▶ *Change the personal pronouns to* we, us *or* our.

6. I worked night and day. _____
7. I worked through lunch breaks. _____
8. These are my qualifications for the project. _____
9. I am glad to do it. _____
10. I always do my best. _____

Personal Success Skill   Sharing Responsibility

▶ *Read this model.*

    Speaker A: You did a good job.

    Speaker B: Thank you. Actually, *we* did a good job. It was a team effort.

▶ *Practice with your classmates.*

Speaker A:	You did a good job. You finished on time. You finished ahead of schedule. You made the sale. You pleased the client. You wrote a good report.

Speaker B: Thank you. Actually, _____ . It was a team effort.

▶ *Study the model:*

Speaker A: What | would you like me to do?
           | do you want me to do?

Speaker B: | I want you to   create the graphs for the proposal.
           | I'd like you to

▶ *Write answers to these questions.*

1. What do you want me to do? (call the client)

   _____

2. What do you want me to do? (survey the competition)

   _____

3. What do you want me to do? (leave a message)

   _____

4. What do you want me to do? (read the report)

   _____

5. What do you want me to do? (copy the letter)

   _____

▶ *Study the conversation.*

Speaker A: What does he want us to do?
Speaker B: He wants us to stay late.

▶ *Write the answers to these questions.*

1. What does she want us to do? (go home)

   _____

2. What does Mr. Barry want me to do? (send the fax)

   _____

3. What does Mrs. Smith want me to do? (finish a letter)

   _____

4. What does Miss Turner want him to do? (stay late)

   _____

5. What does Mr. Joyce want us to do? (leave now)

   _____

Speak for Yourself

▶ *Work with a classmate. One of you is Speaker A; the other is Speaker B. Speaker A will choose a task from the list below. Speaker B will choose an excuse and suggest the name of another employee.*

Speaker A

Tasks:
type this report
create these graphs
survey the competition
meet with the client
copy this proposal
deliver this proposal

Speaker A: Can you **help me with this proposal**?

Speaker B:

Speaker A: I'd really like YOUR help.

Speaker B:

Speaker B

Excuses:
finish this report
call the West coast
go home early
catch a plane
answer a phone call

Speaker A:

Speaker B: I'm sorry. I have to **finish this report**. Maybe **Jane** can help you.

Speaker A:

Speaker B: I would like to, but I just don't have time.
             or
             All right. I'll do it for you.

▶ *Continue with the other options and practice with your classmate. Switch the roles of Speaker A and Speaker B.*

▶ *Read the following letter.*

City Business Association

22 North Street • Seattle, Washington, 10401

October 13, 1994

Mr. John L. Sims, President
PMA Associates
1000 Concord Avenue
Seattle, Washington 10401

Dear Mr. Sims,
    We are pleased to inform you that you have received The Best of
the Best Managers award from the City Business Association for the
year. You will find the award enclosed with the letter.
    Congratulations to you and your employees.

    Sincerely,

    R.J. Carter

    R.J. Carter, President
    City Business Association

Enclosure

▶ *Circle your answer.*

1. Where does Mr. Sims work?
   a. PMA Associates   b. City Business Association
2. Where does Mr. Carter work?
   a. PMA Associates   b. City Business Association
3. Who won the award?
   a. Mr. Sims   b. PMA Associates
4. Who gave the award?
   a. Mr. Sims   b. Mr. Carter
5. Where is the award?
   a. In the envelope   b. At the City Business Association

▶ *Read the model.*

PMA Associates

1000 Concord Avenue
Seattle, Washington 10401
(313) 890-0987

```
October 26, 1994

Mr. R.J. Carter
City Business Association
22 North Street
Seattle, Washington 10401

Dear Mr. Carter:

Thank you so much for your letter.  I am honored to
receive the Best of the Best Managers award.  But I
couldn't have done it by myself.

As you know, PMA Associates hires only the most qualified
employees. All our projects are a team effort.  For this
reason, I will share credit with my employees.

Thank you again for the award.

Sincerely,


John L. Simms

John L. Simms
```

Situation 1: Mrs. Janice Fowler has received a letter from Mr. Cooper. She has received an award for "The Most Successful Seller" of her company.

▶ *Complete the letter. Check the model letter on page 125 if you need help.*

Dear Mr. Carter:

Thank _____ so much for your letter.   I am_____ to receive
the _____ Successful Seller_____.   But I couldn't have done
it_____ myself.
As you know, the company _____ only the most qualified employees.
Our employees make a _____ effort.   For this reason, I will
_____ credit with my employees.
Thank you _____ for the award.

Sincerely,

Mrs. Janice Fowler

Situation 2: Ms. Tina Poole has received a letter from Mrs. Sweeney. Tina has received an award for "The Most Sales" of her company.

▶ *Complete the letter. Check the model letter on page 125 if you need help.*

Dear Mrs. Sweeney:

_____ you so much for your_____.   I am honored to
_____ the Most _____ award.   But I couldn't have done
it by _____ .
As you know, the company hires only the most_____
employees. Our employees make a team _____ .
For this reason, I will share _____ with my employees.
Thank you again for _____ .

Sincerely,

Ms. Tina Poole

Putting It All Together

Planning Ahead

Work in small groups. Make arrangements for one of these situations or one of your own.

- An important client is coming from out-of-town.
- Your company is moving to a new building.

Think of all the tasks and assign them to the group members.

a. What must be done?
b. Who will do it?
c. When will it be done?
d. Who will supervise?

When you are finished, compare your tasks with those from other groups.

Congratulations Are in Order

Work in small groups. Your group will present an award to another group. Decide:
a. What is the award for? Did they finish a project on time? Under budget? Did they win a new client?
b. What kind of award is it? Is it a certificate? A salary increase? Extra vacation?

One member of one group will present the award. Congratulate the group members for 30 seconds without stopping.

A member of the other group will accept the award. Share credit for the award for 30 seconds without stopping.

Other group members will present the awards to (and receive the awards from) other groups.

Step 10 Summary

- Share the credit.
- Be a team player.
- Make your boss look good.
- Congratulate colleagues.

ANSWER KEY

Step 1 Be Positive

Page 2
Set 1: 1. Yes   **2.** Yes   **3.** Answers will vary.   **4.** No   **5.** No   **6.** No   **7.** Yes   **8.** Yes

Set 2: Answers will vary.

Page 3
Set 1: 1. Yes   **2.** Yes   **3.** Maybe   **4.** Yes   **5.** Yes   **6.** Yes

Set 2: 1. Ms. Chapman   **2.** Ms. Chapman   **3.** Answers will vary.   **4.** Mr. Carey   **5.** Answers will vary.   **6.** Answers will vary.

Page 4
1. negative   **2.** negative   **3.** positive   **4.** positive   **5.** middle-of-the-road   **6.** middle-of-the-road
7. positive   **8.** negative

Page 5
1-5. Answers will vary.   **6. Responses:** Give a positive response, make eye contact, smile, and offer your hand; **Why:** All are positive; **What:** Your positive attitude and body language.

Page 6
Set 1:
Polite in Your Country? Answers will vary.
Polite in the U.S.? 1. No   **2.** Yes   **3.** Yes   **4.** Yes   **5.** No   **6.** No   **7.** Yes

Set 2: 1. bad   **2.** not interested   **3.** bad   **4.** interested

Page 7
Answers will vary.

Page 8
Set 1: 1. I want a job.   **2.** I understand.   **3.** I work hard.   **4.** I know your name.   **5.** I make eye contact.   **6.** I sleep well at night.   **7.** I smile.

Set 2: Answers will vary. Sample answers are given.
1. My job is terrific.   **2.** This office is great.   **3.** I make a good impression.   **4.** My co-workers are super.   **5.** The Personnel Director is nice.   **6.** My health is good.   **7.** My attitude is positive.

Page 9
Making eye contact: +   **Tired:** -   **Smiling:** +   **Frowning:** -   **Energetic:** +
Inattentive: -   **Inappropriately dressed:** -   **Appropriately dressed:** +   **Avoiding eye contact:** -
Attentive: +

Page 10
Answers will vary.

Step 2   Be Thoughtful

Page 12
Set 1: 1. Bill   **2.** Mary   **3.** Smith   **4.** Kent   **5.** No   **6.** Yes   **7.** No   **8.** Yes
Set 2: 1. Answers will vary.   **2.** Answers will vary.   **3.** Yes   **4.** Yes

Page 13
Set 1: 1. Jack   **2.** Wright   **3.** Yes   **4.** Yes   **5.** Yes   **6.** Yes

Set 2: 1. Barnes   **2.** Wright   **3-5.** Answers will vary.

Page 14
Set 1: Answers will vary.

Set 2: 1. Quinn; Jennings   **2.** Mr. Hopkins; Ms. White

Page 15
Set 1: Kent; K-E-N-T

Set 2: Answers will vary.

Page 16
Answers will vary.

Page 17
Set 1: Answers will vary.

Set 2: Answers will vary.

Page 18
Set 1: 1. Julie Robins   **2.** Mark Grant   **3.** Rob Jennings   **4.** Bob Grodosky   **5.** Jane Quinn

Set 2: Answers will vary.

Page 19
Answers will vary.

Page 20
1. Are you good with faces?   **2.** Are you from Egypt?   **3.** Are you the new secretary?
4. Are you studying English?   **5.** Are you a salesman?

Page 21
Set 1: 1. Do you speak Chinese?   **2.** Do you study English?   **3.** Do you have a job?
4. Do you like your work?   **5.** Do you have a business card?

Set 2: 1. Where do you work?   **2.** What do you do?   **3.** How do you spell your name?
4. When do you work?   **5.** Where do you study?

Page 22
1. Ken Woods   **2.** Charles Watts   **3.** Charles Watts   **4.** Charles Watts   **5.** Ken Woods

Page 23
you; store; looking; printers; questions

Page 24
Barnes; you; coming; looking; our; computers; have; questions; call; yours

Page 25
1. Introduce Yourself; Ask for Clarification; Ask for the Spelling of the Name; Use the Name; Write the Name down **2-4.** Answers will vary.

Step 3 Be a Team Player

Page 28
Set 1: 1. Yes **2.** No **3.** Yes **4.** No **5.** No **6.** Answers will vary. **7.** Answers will vary. **8.** Answers will vary. **9.** No **10.** Answers will vary.

Set 2: Answers will vary.

Page 29
Set 1: 1. Yes **2.** No **3.** No **4.** Yes **5.** Yes **6.** Yes **7.** No

Set 2: 1. Ron Howard **2.** Mark Curtis **3-5.** Answers will vary.

Page 31
Set 1: 1. b **2.** b **3.** b **4.** a **5.** b

Set 2: 1. The President/CEO **2.** Assistant Manager, Europe **3.** Purchasing Clerk **4.** Personnel Assistant **5.** Vice-President, Administration

Page 33
Set 1: 1. a **2.** the **3.** the **4.** a **5.** a

Set 2: 1. the **2.** the **3.** a **4.** the

Page 34
1. in **2.** for/at **3.** in **4.** in **5.** for/at **6.** for/at

Page 35
Answers will vary.

Pages 36-37
1. a;a **2.** b;a **3.** a;a **4.** a;a **5.** a **6.** a **7.** a **8.** a

Page 38
introduce; order; you; Best; yours

Page 39
Dear; nice; the; last; chance; Thank; invitation; future; Sincerely

Step 4 Be Interested

Page 42
Set 1: 1. Yes **2.** Maybe **3.** Maybe **4.** Maybe **5.** No **6.** Answers will vary. **7.** No **8.** No **9.** Maybe

Set 2: Answers will vary.

Page 43
Set 1: 1. Yes **2.** Yes **3.** Yes **4.** Yes **5.** Yes **6.** Yes **7.** Yes

Set 2: 1. Mr. Patterson   **2.** Mr. Revson   **3.** Ms. Steele   **4.** Golf   **5.** Europe   **6.** Mention European sales.

Page 44
Set 1: 1. Ms. Jones, Mr. Brown. Mr. Brown, Ms. Jones.   **2.** Mr. Williams, Mr. Smith. Mr. Smith, Mr. Williams.   **3.** Ms. Wright, Mr. Reed. Mr. Reed, Ms. Wright.
Set 2: Answers will vary.

Page 46
1. a   **2.** a   **3.** b   **4.** b   **5.** b

Page 47
Set 1: 1. a   **2.** a   **3.** b   **4.** c   **5.** b

Set 2: 1. Where are you going?   **2.** How often do you travel?   **3.** Why do you like New York?   **4.** Who are you going with?   **5.** Which train do you take?

Set 3:
Polite in Your Country? Answers will vary.
Polite in the U.S.? 1. No   **2.** No   **3.** No   **4.** No   **5.** No   **6.** Yes   **7.** No   **8.** No   **9.** Yes   **10.** Yes

Page 48
Set 1: 1. He's an assistant in Personnel.   **2.** She's the Vice-President in Sales and Marketing.
3. He's the Assistant Manager in Domestic Sales.   **4.** She's the Manager in International Sales.
5. He's an accountant in Accounting.

Pages 48-49
Set 2: 1. She's a clerk in Purchasing at Dale Lumber.   **2.** He's a salesman in the Pacific Rim Division at Apple Computer.   **3.** She's the Manager of Domestic Sales at Ford Motors.   **4.** He's a secretary in Personnel at Lockheed Aircraft.   **5.** She's the Vice-President of Administration at Acme Steel.

Set 3: Answers will vary.

Page 50
Set 1: 1. C-1   **2.** A-3   **3.** C-5   **4.** A-1   **5.** B-1

Set 2: Answers will vary.

Page 51
I; announcement; thought; interest

Page 52
saw; brochure; golfing; it; you

Step 5 Be Organized

Page 56
Set 1: 1. Yes   **2.** Maybe   **3.** Yes   **4.** Maybe   **5.** Yes   **6.** No   **7.** Yes

Set 2: Answers will vary.

Page 57
Set 1: 1. Yes   **2.** Yes   **3.** No   **4.** ?   **5.** Yes   **6.** Yes   **7.** Yes   **8.** Yes

Set 2: Answers will vary.

Page 58
1. Breakfast meeting, professional; Tennis, personal; Telephone appt., professional; Meeting, professional **2.** b **3.** a **4.** b **5.** b **6.** a **7.** a **8.** a **9.** b

Page 60
Answers will vary.

Pages 62 - 63
Set 1: 1. at **2.** on **3.** in **4.** in **5.** at

Set 2: Answers will vary.

Set 3: 1. a **2.** a **3.** b

Page 64
Set 1: 1. a **2.** a **3.** a

Set 2: 1. b **2.** a **3.** a

Pages 66-67
Set 1: 1. a **2.** a **3.** a **4.** b **5.** a

Set 2: 1. September; October; November; December; January -February; March; April; May **2.** Jan.; Feb.; Mar.; Apr.; May-June; July; Aug.; Sept.

Set 3: Answers will vary.

Step 6 Be Punctual

Page 70
Set 1: 1. Yes **2.** Yes **3.** Yes **4.** Answers will vary. **5.** No **6.** Yes **7.** Yes **8.** Answers will vary. **9.** No **10.** No

Set 2: Answers will vary.

Page 71
Set 1: 1. Yes **2.** Yes **3.** Yes **4.** No **5.** Yes

Set 2: 1. Mr. King **2.** Ms. Green **3.** Mr. Minor's time **4.** Write an apology to Mr. Minor **5.** Arrive 15 minutes early **6.** Answers will vary.

Page 72
Set 1: 1. Yes **2.** 1:45 **3.** 15 minutes **4.** Harrison **5.** Eight

Set 2: 1-3. Answers will vary. **4.** Wilson, 12:45; Stedman, 1:00; Robinson, 1:45; Foresman, 2:30; Banneck, 3:30; Wood, 4:15; Reid, 5:00; Harrison, 5:45.

Page 73
1. Yes **2.** Maybe **3.** No **4.** Yes **5.** Yes **6.** Yes **7.** Yes **8.** Yes **9.** Maybe **10.** Yes

Page 74
Set 1: 1. P/F **2.** A/W **3.** P/F **4.** P/F **5.** A/W **6.** P/F **7.** A/W **8.** A/W **9.** A/W **10.** A/W

Set 2: 1. No problem. **2.** Answers will vary. **3.** Answers will vary. **4.** No problem. **5.** No problem.
6. Answers will vary.

Page 76
Answers will vary.

Page 77
Set 1: 1. A presentation **2.** 2:00 p.m. **3.** 1:45 p.m. **4.** No

Set 2: 1. A reception **2.** 6:00 p.m. **3.** 6:30 p.m. **4.** Yes **5.** 7:45 p.m.

Page 79
Set 1: am; late; detained; sincere; yours

Set 2: sorry; reception; unavoidably; apologies; Sincerely; (your name)

Step 7 Be Prepared

Page 82
Set 1: 1. Yes **2.** No **3.** Maybe **4.** Maybe **5.** Yes **6.** No

Sets 2 - 3: Answers will vary.

Page 83
Set 1: 1. Yes **2.** Yes **3.** Yes **4.** Maybe **5.** Yes **6.** Yes **7.** Yes **8.** Yes

Set 2: 1. Ms. Reynolds **2.** Mr. Spitz **3.** Ms. Reynolds **4.** Its full of details.

Page 85
1. 20% **2.** 30% **3.** 30% **4.** Salaries

Page 86
1. U.S. $15,000 **2.** U.S. $45,000 **3.** U.S. $5,000 **4.** 4th quarter **5. Print: 1st**: U.S. $55,000; **2nd**: U.S. $80,000; **3rd**: U.S. $120,000; **4th**: U.S. $100,000; **Total Print: $355,000; TV: 1st**: U.S. $95,000; **2nd**: U.S. $95,000; **3rd**: U.S. $35,000; **4th**: U.S. $150,000; **Total TV: $375,000.**

Page 87
1. 400,000 **2.** 100,000 **3.** 500,000 **4.** 450,000 **5.** 1992 **6.** 1993

Page 88
1. How much office space was leased in 1991? **2.** What percentage of the expenses were spent on rent? **3.** How much money was spent on TV advertising in the fourth quarter? **4.** In which quarter was more money spent on advertising?

Page 89
Set 1: 1. One **2.** Two **3.** One **4.** One **5.** One **6.** Two **7.** One

Set 2: 1. There no/is competition. **2.** The Product will cost two million dollars.
3. She gave a thorough proposal. **4.** The new product is interesting. **5.** The report gives a lot of details.

6. I am not sure how much it will cost.   7. The minutes of the meeting matched the agenda.

Set 3: 1. to answer   **2.** to copy   **3.** to make   **4.** to increase

Set 4: 1. I need to answer the phone.   **2.** I need to increase sales.   **3.** I need to make a reservation.
4. I need to make a copy of my report.

Page 90
1. A meeting   **2.** Managers   **3.** In the conference room   **4.** 2 1/2 hours   **5.** January 10
6. Two   **7.** Crane   **8.** No   **9.** 340-7979   **10.** Thursday

Page 91
There will be a planning meeting. "Marketing New Products" on Monday, March 6 at 4:00 p.m. The meeting will be at the Fairview Hotel at 6940 Amherst Avenue. The admission is free. Call (613) 459-6832 for more information.

Page 92
Set 1: There will be a meeting for small business owners, "Sales and Marketing," on Tuesday, July 30 at 1:00 p.m. The meeting will be at the City View Hotel at 960 67th Avenue. The admission is $10. Call (703) 594-7854 for more information.

Set 2: There will be a World Trade Seminar, "New Trade Policy," on Friday, December 12 at 3:30 p.m. at the World Conference Center at Drysdale Circle. The admission is $125. Call (512) 433-3344 for more information.

Step 8 Be Polite

Page 96
Set 1: 1. Yes   **2.** No   **3.** Maybe   **4.** Yes   **5.** Maybe

Set 2: Answers will vary.

Page 97
Set 1: 1. Yes   **2.** No   **3.** Yes   **4.** No   **5.** Yes   **6.** Yes   **7.** Yes

Set 2: 1. Mr. Winston   **2.** Because he is polite.   **3.** He often calls Mr. Green and talks with Barbara.
4. Mr. Winston   **5.** Mr. Winston   **6.** Mr. Winston   **7.** Answers will vary.

Page 99
Set 1: 1. e   **2.** a   **3.** b   **4.** f   **5.** c   **6.** d

Set 2: 1. b   **2.** b   **3.** b   **4.** b   **5.** b

Page 101
1. asking   **2.** Thank you for coming.   **3.** Thank you for helping.   **4.** Thank you for asking.
5. Thank you for calling.

Page 102
Set 1: 1. Yes   **2.** Yes   **3.** No   **4.** No   **5.** Maybe   **6.** Yes   **7.** Yes   **6.** Yes

Pages 103-104
Answers will vary.

Page 105
Identify yourself; State your purpose; Suggest alternatives

Step 9 Be Patient

Page 108
Set 1: 1. Yes   **2.** Maybe   **3.** No   **4.** No   **5.** No   **6.** No   **7.** Yes

Set 2: Answers will vary.

Page 109
Set 1: 1. No   **2.** Yes   **3.** Yes   **4.** No   **5.** Yes

Set 2: 1. Mr. Decker   **2.** Answers will vary.   **3.** Mr. Decker   **4-6.** Answers will vary.

Page 110
Set 1: 1. d   **2.** b   **3.** c   **4.** a

Set 2: 1. Thanks for staying late. I really appreciate it.   **2.** Thanks for meeting me. I really appreciate it.
3. Thanks for coming early. I really appreciate it.   **4.** Thanks for working overtime. I really appreciate it.

Page 111
Set 1: 1. Could you please reprint this report?   **2.** Could you please retype this?   **3.** Could you please reread this?   **4.** Could you please redo this?   **5.** Could you please rewrite this?

Set 2: 1. a   **2.** b   **3.** b   **4.** a

Page 112
Set 1: 1. b   **2.** b   **3.** b   **4.** b

Set 2: 1. Speaker A: The wrong name was written on this letter. Speaker B: Im sorry. Ill rewrite it.
2. Speaker A: The wrong customer was called. Speaker B: Im sorry. Ill call again.   **3.** Speaker A: The wrong letter was sent. Speaker B: Im sorry. Ill send it again.   **4.** Speaker A: The copy was bad. Speaker B: Im sorry. Ill copy it again.   **5.** Speaker A: Two typos were made in this letter. Speaker B: Im sorry. Ill retype it.

Page 113
1. b   **2.** a   **3.** b   **4.** b   **5.** a

Page 114
1. We should talk about the problem.   **2.** He should know her name.   **3.** I should finish the report.
4. Mrs. Vernon should call right now.   **5.** The manager should write an agenda.

Page 115
Set 1: Please; date; retype; Mary Clark

Set 2: note; total; Could; redo; Frank Nance

Page 116
Set a positive tone/give a compliment; Show the mistake; Make a polite suggestion.

Step 10 Be Loyal

Page 118
Set 1: 1. Maybe **2.** Maybe **3.** No **4.** Maybe **5.** Maybe **6.** No **7.** Maybe

Set 2: Answers will vary.

Page 119
Set 1: 1. Yes **2.** No **3.** Yes **4.** No **5.** Yes **6.** No **7.** Yes

Set 2: 1. Ms. King **2.** Ms. King **3-5.** Answers will vary. **6.** Ms. King **7.** Answers will vary.

Page 120
Set 1: 1. Taking **2.** Sharing **3.** Sharing **4.** Sharing **5.** Sharing **6.** Taking **7.** Taking
8. Sharing **9.** Sharing **10.** Sharing

Set 2: Answers will vary.

Page 121
Set 1: 1. We did it all ourselves. **2.** To do a job right, let us do it. **3.** We finished ahead of schedule.
4. We made the sale ourselves. **5.** It was our report that won the client. **6.** We worked night and day.
7. We worked through lunch breaks. **8.** These are our qualifications for the project.
9. We are glad to do it. **10.** We always do our best.

Page 122
Set 1: 1. I want you to call the client. **2.** I want you to survey the competition. **3.** I want you to leave a message. **4.** I want you to read the report. **5.** I want you to copy the letter.

Set 2: 1. She wants us to go home. **2.** He wants me to send the fax. **3.** She wants me to finish a letter. **4.** She wants him to stay late. **5.** He wants us to leave now.

Page 124
1. a **2.** b **3.** a **4.** b **5.** a

Page 126
Set 1: you; honored; Most; award; by; hires; team; share; again

Set 2: Thank; letter; receive; Sales; myself; qualified; effort; credit; the award